1 Widening horizon
2 Fusion of horizons
3 Disseminating horizons

Acts of Faith

Acts of Faith ❧

The Story of an American Muslim,
the Struggle for the Soul of a Generation

Eboo Patel

Beacon Press
Boston

Beacon Press
25 Beacon Street
Boston, Massachusetts 02108-2892
www.beacon.org

Beacon Press books
are published under the auspices of   ·
the Unitarian Universalist Association of Congregations.

14 13 12 11   8 7 6 5 4 3 2

This book is printed on acid-free paper that meets the uncoated paper
ANSI/NISO specifications for permanence as revised in 1992.

Composition by Wilsted & Taylor Publishing Services

Library of Congress Cataloging-in-Publication Data

Patel, Eboo.
  Acts of faith : the story of an American Muslim, the struggle for the soul of a
generation / Eboo Patel.
    p. cm.
  Includes bibliographical references.
  ISBN 978-0-8070-0622-1
  1. Patel, Eboo. 2. Muslims—United States—Biography. 3. East Indian
Americans—Biography. 4. Muslims—United States—Ethnic identity.
5. United States—Ethnic relations. 6. Pluralism (Social sciences)—United
States. 7. Interfaith Youth Core. 8. United States—Religious life and customs.
9. Youth—United States—Religious life. 10. Religions—Relations. I. Title.

E184.M88P38 2007
305.6'97089914073—dc22
[B]   2007009064

To the teachers, to the storytellers

I am large, I contain multitudes.
WALT WHITMAN

The roar of Creation
Resolves into music.
RABINDRANATH TAGORE

Start a huge, foolish project,
like Noah.
RUMI

Contents

Introduction: The Faith Line

Someone who doesn't make flowers makes thorns.
If you're not building rooms where wisdom can be
openly spoken, you're building a prison.

SHAMS OF TABRIZ

Eric Rudolph is in court pleading guilty. But he is not sorry. Not for the radio-controlled nail bomb that he detonated at New Woman All Women Health Care in Birmingham, Alabama, that killed an off-duty police officer and left a nurse hobbled and half-blind. Not for the bomb at the 1996 Olympics in Atlanta that killed one, injured dozens, and sent shock waves of fear through the global community. Not for his hate-spitting letter stating, "We declare and will wage total war on the ungodly communist regime in New York and your legislative bureaucratic lackeys in Washington," signed "the Army of God." Not for defiling the Holy Bible by writing "bomb" in the margin of his copy.

In fact, Rudolph is proud and defiant. He lectures the judge on the righteousness of his actions. He gloats as he recalls federal agents passing within steps of his hiding place. He unabashedly states that abortion, homosexuality, and all hints of "global socialism" still need to be "ruthlessly opposed." He does this in the name of Christianity, quot-

ing from the New Testament: "I have fought the good fight, I have finished my course, I have kept the faith."

Felicia Sanderson lost her husband, Robert, a police officer, to
Rudolph's Birmingham bomb. During the sentencing hearing, she
played a tape of speeches made at her husband's funeral. People remembered him keeping candy for children in his patrol car and raising money to replace Christmas gifts for a family whose home had
been robbed. Felicia Sanderson pointed to Rudolph and told the
court, "He has been responsible for every tear my sons have shed."

Judge C. Lynwood Smith sentenced Rudolph to two life terms,
compared him to the Nazis, and said that he was shocked at Rudolph's
lack of remorse. But many others felt a twitch of pride.

Eric Rudolph might have been a loner, but he did not act alone.
He was produced by a movement and encouraged by a culture. In
the woods of western North Carolina, where Rudolph evaded federal
agents for five years, people cheered him on, helped him hide, made
T-shirts that said RUN RUDOLPH RUN. The day he was finally caught, a
woman from the area was quoted as saying, "Rudolph's a Christian and
I'm a Christian ... Those are our values. These are our woods."

Of all the information published about Rudolph, one sentence in
particular stood out to me: Rudolph wrote an essay denying the Holocaust when he was in high school. How does a teenager come to hold
such a view?

The answer is simple: people taught him. Eric Rudolph had always
had trouble in school—fights, truancy. He never quite fit in. His father died when he was young. His mother met and followed a series
of dangerous iconoclasts who preached a theology of hate. The first
was Tom Branham, who encouraged the Rudolph family to move next
door to him in Topton, North Carolina. Eric was soon drawing Nazi
symbols in his schoolbooks at nearby Nantahala High School. Next,
Eric's mother moved the family to Schell City, Missouri, to be near
Dan Gayman, a leading figure in the extremist Christian Identity
movement. Gayman had been a high school principal and knew how
to make his mark on young people. He assumed a fatherly relationship

with Eric, enrolled him in Christian Identity youth programs, and made sure he read the literature of the movement. Gayman taught Eric that the Bible was the history of Aryan whites and that Jews were the spawn of Satan and part of a tribe called the "the mud people." The world was nearing a final struggle between God's people and Satan's servants, and it was up to the "conscious" Aryans to ensure victory for the right race. Eric took to calling the television "the Electric Jew." He carved swastikas into his mother's living room furniture. His library included virulently anti-Semitic publications such as *The Protocols of the Learned Elders of Zion, Anne Frank's Diary: A Hoax,* and *The International Jew.* Under the tutelage of Gayman and other radical preachers, Eric Rudolph's hate did what hate always does: it spread.

I imagine these preachers felt a surge of pride when Rudolph responded to Judge Smith's question about whether he set off the bomb in Birmingham with a smug, "I certainly did."

Middle school students in Whitwell, Tennessee, are giving tours of one of the most profound Holocaust memorials anywhere in the world: a German railcar that was used to transport Jews to Auschwitz. The young people ask guests to imagine how it might feel to be one of the seventy or eighty Jews packed into that tight space, hearing the wheels clanking as the train took them to torture and death. They explain that the railcar is filled with millions of paper clips, each one a symbol of a Jew murdered by the Nazis. One student says that to see a paper clip now is to think of a soul. The sign at the entrance of the memorial reads: "We ask you to pause and reflect on the evil of intolerance and hatred." The sign on the way out states: "What can I do to spread the message of love and tolerance these children have demonstrated with this memorial?"

One Whitwell student tour guide, about to graduate from eighth grade, reflects, "In the future, when I come back and see it, knowing that I was here to do this, it will be not just a memory, but kind of like in your heart, that you've changed the way that people think about other people."

Whitwell is a town of fewer than two thousand residents, located outside Chattanooga in the coal mining region of southeastern Tennessee, about a hundred miles from where the Ku Klux Klan was born. It has two traffic lights and a whole lot of GOD BLESS AMERICA signs. The mines closed thirty years ago, leaving the region even poorer than it was before. You can count the number of black and Latino families in Whitwell on two hands, and you won't need any of those fingers to count the number of Catholics, Jews, and Muslims, because there aren't any.

Why would white Protestant kids in a poor region with a history of prejudice care so much about educating people about Judaism? The answer is simple: people taught them. The principal of Whitwell Middle School, Linda Hooper, wanted the students in her school to learn about cultures and people who are different from themselves. "Our children, they are respectful; they are thoughtful; they are caring. But they are pretty much homogeneous. When we come up to someone who is not like us, we don't have a clue."

She sent a teacher to a diversity conference, and he came back with the idea of a Holocaust education project. "This was *our* need," Hooper said.

Over the next several years, the students at Whitwell studied that horrible time, met with Holocaust survivors, learned about the rich tradition of Judaism, and taught all the people they touched about the powerful role that young people can play in advocating for pluralism.

Lena Gitter, a ninety-five-year-old Holocaust survivor, heard about the project and wrote the students a letter: "I witnessed what intolerance and indifference can lead to. I am thankful that late in life I can see and hear that the teaching of tolerance is alive and well and bears fruit. When you ask the young, they will do the right thing. With tears in my eyes, I bow my head before you. Shalom."

Eric Rudolph and the young people of Whitwell are two very different responses to one of the most important questions of our time: in a world of passionate religiosity and intense interaction, how will people from different faith backgrounds engage one another? Rudolph responded to people who were different by building bombs of destruction. The students of Whitwell responded to diversity by building bridges of understanding. Rudolph is a religious totalitarian. The students of Whitwell are religious pluralists. They are on different sides of the faith line.

One hundred years ago, the great African American scholar W. E. B. Du Bois famously said, "The problem of the twentieth century is the problem of the color line." I believe that the twenty-first century will be shaped by the question of the faith line. On one side of the faith line are the religious totalitarians. Their conviction is that only one interpretation of one religion is a legitimate way of being, believing, and belonging on earth. Everyone else needs to be cowed, or converted, or condemned, or killed. On the other side of the faith line are the religious pluralists, who hold that people believing in different creeds and belonging to different communities need to learn to live together. Religious pluralism is neither mere coexistence nor forced consensus. It is a form of proactive cooperation that affirms the identity of the constituent communities while emphasizing that the well-being of each and all depends on the health of the whole. It is the belief that the common good is best served when each community has a chance to make its unique contribution.

Disagree w/ this dichotomy

Religious totalitarians have the unique advantage of being able to oppose each other and work together at the same time. Osama bin Laden says that Christians are out to destroy Muslims. Pat Robertson says that Muslims want only to dominate Christians. Bin Laden points to Pat Robertson as evidence of his case. Robertson points to bin Laden as proof of his. Bin Laden says he is moving Muslims to his side of the faith line. Robertson claims he is moving Christians to his. But if you look from a certain angle, you see that they are not on opposite sides at all. They are right next to each other, standing shoulder to shoulder, a most unlikely pair, two totalitarians working collectively against the dream of a common life together.

The outcome of the question of the faith line depends on which side young people choose. Young people have always played a key role in social movements, from the struggle against apartheid in South Africa to the rise of the Nazi Party in Germany. We live in an era where the populations of the most religiously volatile areas of the world are strikingly young. Seventy-five percent of India's one billion plus are not yet twenty-five. Eighty-five percent of the people who live in the Palestinian territories are under age thirty-three. More than two-thirds of the people of Iran are under age thirty. The median age in Iraq is nineteen and a half. All of these people are standing on the faith line. Whose message are they hearing?

Watching *Paper Clips,* the documentary film made about the Whitwell students, I could not help but wonder: What if Linda Hooper had gotten to Eric Rudolph before Dan Gayman did? What if Rudolph had attended the First United Methodist Church in Whitwell, which hosted the events for the Holocaust project, instead of Christian Identity youth programs, had helped collect paper clips with the other kids at Whitwell Middle School instead of studying with bigots, had read *Anne Frank: The Diary of a Young Girl* instead of *Anne Frank's Diary: A Hoax?* Eric Rudolph the religious terrorist was not inevitable, just as the teenage bridge builders of Whitwell were not. They were each carefully and intentionally nurtured.

This is a book about how some young people become champions of religious pluralism while others become the foot soldiers of religious totalitarianism. Its thesis is simple: influences matter, programs count, mentors make a difference, institutions leave their mark. When we look back in the lives of young religious terrorists, we find a web of individuals and organizations that shaped them. These young killers are not, for the most part, dramatically deranged individuals. They are kids who fell into murderously manipulative hands. Every time we see a teenager kill someone in the name of God, we should picture a pair of shadowy hands behind him, showing him how to make the bomb or point the gun, giving him a manual with the prayers to say while committing murder, steadying his shaking hands with callused, steely ones, blessing him as he resolves to do the deed. And then we should ask: why weren't the hands of people who care about pluralism shaping that kid instead of the hands of religious totalitarians?

Religious extremism is a movement of young people taking action. Hindu nationalists, hate-filled rabbis, Christian Identity preachers, and Muslim totalitarians prey on young people's desire to have a clear identity and make a powerful impact. We see their successes in the headlines of our newspapers every day.

Interfaith cooperation is too often a conference of senior religious leaders talking. No doubt these leaders play a crucial role in religious bridge building. They have broken important theological ground, articulated frameworks for interfaith understanding, and sent the signal that cooperation with the religious Other is not only possible but necessary. Yet few in my generation have been involved.

I am an American Muslim from India. My adolescence was a series of rejections, one after another, of the various dimensions of my heritage, in the belief that America, India, and Islam could not coexist within the same being. If I wanted to be one, I could not be the others. My struggle to understand the traditions I belong to as mutually enriching rather than mutually exclusive is the story of a generation of young people standing at the crossroads of inheritance and discovery, trying to look both ways at once. There is a strong connection between finding a sense of inner coherence and developing a commitment to pluralism. And that has everything to do with who meets you at the crossroads.

When I was in college, I had the sudden realization that all of my heroes were people of deep faith: Dorothy Day, the Dalai Lama, Martin Luther King Jr., Mahatma Gandhi, Malcolm X, the Aga Khan. Moreover, they were all of different faiths. A little more research revealed two additional insights. First, religious cooperation had been central to the work of most of these faith heroes. The Reverend Martin Luther King Jr. partnered with Rabbi Abraham Joshua Heschel in the struggle for civil rights. Mahatma Gandhi stated that Hindu-

Muslim unity was just as important to him as a free India. Second, each of my faith heroes assumed an important leadership role at a young age. King was only twenty-six years old when he led the Montgomery bus boycott. Gandhi was even younger when he started his movement against unjust laws in early-twentieth-century South Africa.

I attended my first interfaith conference when I was twenty-one and discovered that I was the youngest person there by some thirty years. The more conferences I went to, the more I found that general pattern held true. I could not help but reflect upon the young King in Montgomery or the young Gandhi in Johannesburg. I knew my generation had faith heroes of courage and vision. Why weren't they more visibly involved in the crucial project of building religious pluralism, resurrecting the tradition of Gandhi and King in a global era characterized by religious conflict? The faces of religious fanatics were young; the faces of interfaith cooperation were old. Something had to change.

Change happens internally before it takes place in the world. My transformation was catalyzed by a moment of failure.

In high school, the group I ate lunch with included a Cuban Jew, a Nigerian Evangelical, and an Indian Hindu. We were all devout to a degree, but we almost never talked about our religions with one another. Often somebody would announce at the table that he couldn't eat a certain kind of food, or any food at all, for a period of time. We all knew religion hovered behind this, but nobody ever offered any explanation deeper than "my mom said," and nobody ever asked for one.

This silent pact relieved all of us. We were not equipped with a language that allowed us to explain our faith to others or to ask about anyone else's. Back then, I thought little about the dangers lurking within this absence.

A few years after we graduated, my Jewish friend reminded me of a dark time during our adolescence. There were a group of kids in our high school who, for several weeks, took up scrawling anti-Semitic slurs on classroom desks and making obscene statements about Jews in the hallways. I did not confront them. I did not comfort my Jewish friend. I knew little about what Judaism meant to him, less about the emotional effects of anti-Semitism, and next to nothing about how to stop religious bigotry. So I averted my eyes and avoided my friend, because I couldn't stand to face him.

A few years later, he described to me the fear he had experienced coming to school those days, and his utter loneliness as he had watched his close friends simply stand by. Hearing him recount his suffering and my complicity is the single most humiliating experience of my life. I did not know it in high school, but my silence was betrayal: betrayal of Islam, which calls upon Muslims to be courageous and compassionate in the face of injustice; betrayal of America, a nation that relies on its citizens to hold up the bridges of pluralism when others try to destroy them; betrayal of India, a country that has too often seen blood flow in its cities and villages when extremists target minorities and others fail to protect them.

My friend needed more than my silent presence at the lunch table. Pluralism is not a default position, an autopilot mode. Pluralism is an intentional commitment that is imprinted through action. It requires deliberate engagement with difference, outspoken loyalty to others, and proactive protection in the breach. You have to *choose* to step off the faith line onto the side of pluralism, and then you have to make your voice heard. To follow Robert Frost, it is easy to see the death of pluralism in the fire of a suicide bombing. But the ice of silence will kill it just as well.

This is a story of returning to faith, of finding coherence, of committing to pluralism, and of the influences I owe my life to.

I
The Crossroads of the Identity Crisis

> One can only face in others what one can face
> in oneself. On this confrontation depends the
> measure of our wisdom and compassion. This
> energy is all that one finds in the rubble of
> vanished civilizations, and the only hope for ours.
> JAMES BALDWIN, *Nobody Knows My Name*

Hasib Hussain, left hand hanging slightly out of the pocket of his jeans, shuffles into the Luton railway station just before 7:30 a.m. on July 7, 2005, wearing an indifferent expression on his face and a pack on his back. Three young men accompany him. They look like any other group of young people heading for a day touring the museums and art galleries of London. They all wear indifferent expressions. They all wear packs on their backs.

But it is not water bottles and summer novels that they carry. Instead, each pack contains a carefully mixed concoction of hair bleach, food preservatives, and heating chemicals.

Hasib Hussain's pack is the last to blow. It detonates at 9:47 a.m. on a double-decker bus near Tavistock Square, peeling the top off and killing Hasib and thirteen others. Hasib was eighteen years old.

An hour earlier, at the Russell Square Tube station a few blocks away, Germaine Lindsay detonated his pack. It was the deadliest of the four bombings, destroying the lead carriage of the southbound 311 train and killing twenty-six people plus the bomber. Germaine was nineteen years old.

The other two blasts occurred within seconds of the Russell Square explosion. Mohammad Sidique Khan sat on Circle Line train 216. Seconds after it left Edgware Road, traveling west to Paddington, the explosives on his back tore apart his car like a can opener and impacted an oncoming eastbound train. Six people plus Mohammad were killed. Mohammad was thirty.

On the other side of central London, in the heavily Muslim East End, Shehzad Tanweer blew himself up on a westbound Circle Line train leaving Liverpool Street station for Aldgate. When the lights came on, the floor of the train was full of people covered in blood. Seven people plus the bomber were killed. Shehzad was twenty-two.

Shahara Islam was the first of the dead to be buried. A twenty-year-old British-born Bengali Muslim, she was riding the No. 30 bus on her way to her job as a cashier at the Co-operative Bank, Angel branch. I cannot help but imagine her smiling at her murderer, the tall and endearingly awkward Hasib Hussain, when he climbed aboard weighed down by the death in his backpack. The two should have been friends, discussing the challenges of being second-generation South Asian Muslims living between the tawdry permissiveness of British youth culture and the traditionalist piety of their parents' homes. "Our dear daughter is returning to her Lord a bloodstained martyr," her parents said during the funeral. Seven thousand mourners—Muslim and Christian, Jewish and Hindu, Sikh and Zoroastrian —were whispering prayers.

The world lives in London, and when bombs go off, it dies there. Ghanian-born Gladys Wundowa was riding the No. 30 bus on her way from her cleaning job at University College London to a class in housing management. Giles Hart, a British Telecom employee, had held voluntary posts ranging from chair of the Polish Solidarity Campaign of Great Britain to vice chair of the British Humanist Association. He was an activist in the peace movement and a member of the Anti-Slavery Society. His family released a statement that read, "It is tragic that he fell victim to the very evil against which he had struggled." Anthony Fatayi-Williams, Nigerian by heritage, born of a Christian mother and a Muslim father, was also murdered on the bus. An engineering executive by trade, he was passionate about reconciliation in his native Nigeria. "How many mothers' hearts must be maimed?" Anthony's mother asked in a speech she gave after the bombing.

Terry McDermott opens *Perfect Soldiers*, his book on the September 11 hijackers, with the image of Mohamed Atta, the suspected leader of the group, padding around his Hamburg, Germany, apartment in blue flip-flops. It seems so incongruous that this slight loner could have been responsible for the deaths of nearly three thousand Americans and foreign nationals and the profound shift in international affairs that followed. "We want our monsters to be outsized, monstrous," writes McDermott. "We expect them to be somehow equal to their crimes." But the world is a peculiar place, and McDermott, after conducting the definitive study into the lives of the nineteen hijackers, was forced to conclude, "The men of September 11 were, regrettably, I think, fairly ordinary men."

So were the men of July 7, 2005. "Suspects' Neighbors Say There Was No Hint of Evil" was the title of the story in the *New York Times*. Shehzad Tanweer, the twenty-two-year-old Aldgate bomber, loved Elvis Presley's version of Eddy Arnold's song "Make the World Go Away." "I thought his only interest was cricket," Shehzad's uncle said, anguished face still expressing disbelief. Shehzad worked in his father's successful fish and chips shop and drove around town in the family's red Mercedes. He wore brand-name clothes, worked out regularly, and studied sports science at Leeds Metropolitan University. Friends described him as infinitely likable, more apt to talk about sports and cars than anything else.

Mohammad Sidique Khan was a learning mentor at Hillside Primary School. He was universally appreciated by parents, students, and faculty for his commitment to assisting the newly immigrated children with everything from school lessons to athletics. As a teenager, he went by the nickname Sid and wore cowboy boots, expressions of his fascination with all things American. As he grew older, he was the guy young South Asians and Muslims in Leeds would go to if they needed help. "He gave me good advice, had a good head on his shoulders," a young man from the neighborhood told the *New York Times*. "He was rational." Khan's wife was an advocate for moderate Islam and women's rights, and his mother-in-law had received an honor from Queen Elizabeth for her community work.

Germaine Lindsay was described as one of the cool kids in school —smart, funny, and always smiling. Born in Jamaica, he converted to Islam at age fifteen. He became well known for his recitations of the Qur'an at the Leeds Grand Mosque and his robust efforts to convert his classmates. Germaine married a white British Muslim convert, and the two had a baby together. Neither his mother nor his wife could believe that he had become a suicide bomber. His mother remembered Germaine mourning the victims of September 11, and his wife would not accept that Germaine had left her and their baby behind.

Hasib Hussain was the youngest, the shyest, the least remarkable, the most impressionable. When he was a child, Hasib bought his candy from Ajmal Singh's corner shop, like all the other kids in Holbeck, an ethnically mixed neighborhood in the British city of Leeds. He went to primary school a block from his home, and he loved kicking a plastic soccer ball down the street where he lived. His father worked in a factory, and his tight-knit extended family had been in the area for thirty years. It was his mother's call to the police, reporting that Hasib had not returned home from his trip to London with friends and was not answering his cell phone, that broke the bombing case open.

Tall and lanky, Hasib Hussain tried hard to fade into the background at Matthew Murray High School, but the white toughs picked on him anyway. The sermons at the local mosque rarely addressed this reality. His parents' advice was to pray more and do better in school. He started running with a group of Pakistani Muslims who fought back, a crowd that provided him with support and identity but was estranged from the pious Muslim community of his household and mosque. Scared that their son was losing his way, his parents sent him abroad, thinking that religious influence from the Muslim world would straighten him out.

A cousin observed that Hasib returned not only more devout but also more political and strident in his views. "I thought he had been brainwashed," the cousin told the *Guardian*. Hasib began spending more time with Mohammad Sidique Khan. Khan had recently rejected Leeds's mosques for practicing what he claimed was a diluted and false form of Islam and had become part of the inner circle at the Iqra Learning Center.

When radical Muslims traveled through Leeds to spread their message of proper Muslim behavior plus hatred for the West, they held their meetings at the Iqra Learning Center. In addition to traditional Islamic literature like the Qur'an, the Hadith, and books on Muslim law, the store carried materials on Western conspiracy theories against Islam. Part of the collection included DVDs showing scenes of Muslims being maimed and murdered in the Middle East, the Balkans, and Chechnya juxtaposed against President George Bush saying the word "crusade." "It was slick and really made you feel angry," Amear Ali, a thirty-six-year-old Muslim who lives in Leeds told the Associated Press. Ali described how the owner of the bookstore approached him with the offer of religious education lessons. First came the proper way to do Muslim prayers, then the lectures about injustice against Muslims around the world, and next the DVDs. "You could see how it could turn someone to raw hate ... I know it was propaganda and was made to make you feel this way. But what about young guys who see this material as a call to do something?"

That is exactly what Sheikh Omar Bakri Mohammad wants. A

Syrian-born middle-aged father of seven, he lived in North London for nearly two decades, supported in part by a monthly British welfare check of more than $500, before decamping for the Middle East soon after the London bombings. He helped establish Hizb ut-Tahrir, whose mission is to reestablish the Islamic caliphate. In its study circles, Hizb recruits learn that Muslim identity is necessarily opposed to the West. The 2003 Hizb conference in Birmingham, England, drew eight thousand people, many of them young. Zeyno Baran, director of international security and energy programs at the Nixon Center (a nonpartisan foreign policy institution in the United States), said, "Hizb produces thousands of manipulated brains, which then 'graduate' from Hizb and become members of groups like al-Qa'ida . . . It acts like a conveyor belt for terrorists." Sheikh Omar left Hizb, or was asked to leave, after he stated that British prime minister John Major should be assassinated and beheaded for his role in the Gulf War of 1990–1991. After Sheikh Omar's departure, Hizb attempted to refashion itself as a nonviolent organization committed to a puritan Muslim vision.

Unable to preach violence through Hizb, Sheikh Omar went on to organize a radical Muslim youth organization that he called Al-Muhajiroun in the early 1990s. He used this platform to preach sermons and post web messages calling young British Muslims to wage jihad against the West in Iraq, Israel, and Chechnya. He referred to the September 11 hijackers as the Magnificent 19. A poster advertising an Al-Muhajiroun event had pictures of each hijacker set against a glorious, glowing backdrop. Sheikh Omar blamed British foreign policy for the July 7 attacks and said of the hundreds of young British Muslims who attend his sermons, "They know that the Prime Minister has his hands full of the blood of Muslims in Palestine and in Iraq and in Afghanistan. We hear from many who say they want to attack."

Sheikh Omar is a master institution builder and youth organizer. He understands precisely what buttons to push to harden a young Muslim's fluid religious identity into a terrorist commitment. The itinerant Muslim preachers who inspired the radical study circle at the Iqra Learning Center and the locals who organized it likely learned their trade through Sheikh Omar's networks.

How did awkward, shy Hasib Hussain become a suicide bomber? Sheikh Omar's people got to him before we did.

After the flurry of phone calls to friends and family and the relief that they were safe, after the prayers that my wife and I said for the victims and all those left wounded by their loss, I thanked God for saving my skin again. In my life, religious violence has always existed in the gray area between reality and imagination. My cousins in Bombay describe locking themselves inside their apartments in 1993 as Hindu mobs armed with machetes roamed the streets looking for Muslims to kill. My aunt tells about the cold fear that struck her heart when she heard the loud blast that was the Al Qaeda bombing of the American Embassy in Nairobi in 1998. Her husband, a diplomat, had left for work a few minutes before. She thanked God for weeks that his journey to the center of the city had been delayed that day. In November 1999, I left late for an appointment at a waterfront café in Cape Town, South Africa. As I approached, I started noticing glass shards strewn around, and then I heard the wailing sirens. "What's going on?" I asked a cop. "A bomb went off at a pizza parlor," he responded. It was next door to the café where I was supposed to meet a friend.

I practically lived in London for three years. It was where I did the research for my doctorate. I have fond memories and a clear picture of each of the sites that was bombed. Edgware Road and Aldgate had the best kebab stands in the city. Tavistock Square was my favorite park, full of antiwar memorials. I rode the elevator at the Russell Square Tube several times a year and walked the few blocks to the British Museum, where I would stand in front of the Elgin Marbles hoping that the genius of the ancients would provide inspiration for my thesis.

Tavistock Square may never offer the same calm. The Circle Line may never feel normal again. It will be impossible to ride the elevator at Russell Square without remembering the people killed below. All changed forever by four young men who prayed in the same language I consider holy.

An eerie feeling crept over me as I stared at the faces of the London bombers, especially the three who traced their history back to the sub-continent. Their travails in school, their relationships with their parents, their indifference to Islam as adolescents followed by an intense reengagement—it all felt familiar. I sensed a flicker of recognition from a deep place. A piece of their story was a part of me.

I can imagine going to Hasib Hussain's home for dinner. I would have given salaams to his father at the door, taken my shoes off, admired the Qur'anic calligraphy and the picture of the Ka'aba, the most important site in Islam, on the wall. I would have immediately known the curries his mother was cooking from the smells wafting through the house. When I complimented her dinner, she would have looked away shyly, but not before a happy smile crossed her face. I would have sat with Hasib's father in the living room after dinner, drinking Indian masala tea—sweet with sugar, spicy with cinnamon, fragrant with cardamom. We would have made the obligatory comments about global politics, wondering when India and Pakistan would finally work out the issue of Kashmir. Perhaps his father, his Muslim solidarity flaring for an instant, would have told me how angry he was at America for ignoring the plight of the Palestinians for so long and for believing that you can bomb countries into democracy. Then he would have hurriedly said, "But I love the American people. It is the government that does all the bombing."

Inevitably, we would have settled on the subject of life in the West. He would have shaken his head and said that England is hard. You can make a living, yes, but the culture is a stranger to you, and then it takes your son and makes him a stranger, too. He would have told me that all he wanted was for his son to marry a nice Muslim girl, have a family, and make a good living. "I think computers is the best profession nowadays," he would have mused, twisting the ends of his mustache. Then his voice would have fallen a little, and he would have confessed the problems that Hasib had had at school— the falling grades, the truancy, the fights. He would have sounded confused about why. Where was the famed education and social mobility of the West? And then he would have spoken about how sending Hasib abroad had straightened him out. He now wore a Muslim cap and prayed regularly, and he no longer went around with those boys who, rumor had it, were into alcohol and worse things.

The only problem was that Hasib didn't want to go to the local mosque anymore. In fact, he had taken to insulting it. His new friends had started praying at the Iqra Learning Center. Hasib came home from there with books and DVDs, and he spent all his free time reviewing that material. There must be something in there like a firecracker. Now, when he made offhand comments about the plight of Muslims elsewhere, Hasib grew furious and spit out angry words about the West and the importance of returning Islam to power. Hasib's father would have asked me, a few years older than Hasib and also a second-generation South Asian Muslim in the West, if I understood what his son was going through.

I would have swallowed hard.

I know his son's anger in a dangerous way. I remember feigning illness so I could stay home from school as a teenager, afraid to tell my mother the truth: that a group of white kids in gym class had taken to cornering me in the locker room, tearing off my shorts, and hitting me with wet towels, all the while shouting "sand nigger" and "curry maker." When I finally crumpled in a corner, covered with welts, they raced upstairs to tell their girlfriends what they had done to "the Hindu." After I finally got myself together and limped into class, the gym teacher would yell at me for being late and pal around with my tormentors as if he was in on the torture. The girls would snicker and refuse to stand next to me during volleyball, telling their boyfriends, "You never said he smelled *this* bad."

My parents, as loving as they were, simply could not relate to my reality. My mother was convinced that if I would only raise my math grade, the other kids would respect me. "Say your *tasbih*," she would add, referring to the Muslim prayer beads. It made me feel worse to tell her what happened in school, so I stopped. Plus, my parents were never home. My father hated his job in corporate advertising and was looking for a way out, and my mother had recently become a certified public accountant (CPA) and was still getting accustomed to the challenges of balancing professional and family life. My brother and I were left to fend for ourselves.

I was surprised to hear my father shouting at the television screen during the Gulf War of 1990–1991. He had been a strong Reagan supporter during the 1980s and had had only two words for 1988 Democratic presidential candidate Michael Dukakis: "idiot liberal." But he could not contain his fury at President George H. W. Bush. "Say the name of the country right," he would yell every time Bush gave the *I* in "Iraq" the wrong inflection. He was beside himself when Bush, after he had indicated to the Shia and Kurds that the U.S. military would come to their aid if they attempted to overthrow Saddam Hussein, announced while playing golf that he didn't think sending the American military to Baghdad was the right thing to do, knowing full well that this meant certain death for the Muslims who had trusted him. "Muslims are dying by the thousands, and these people don't give a shit," my father would bellow.

And then Bosnia. My father was glued to international news and would regale me with stories and images of the horror abroad every chance he got. "They are using rape as a tool of war, and the strongest military in the world is doing nothing," he would shout. Eyes popping, he would turn to me and say, "What if the neighbors came over and tied you up and made you watch as they killed me and raped your mother, and there was a policeman on the corner doing nothing? That is exactly what is happening in Bosnia, and America is that idle policeman."

My father had always been knowledgeable about world affairs but never active in them. He is a profoundly decent man with a strong personal spirituality, but he was never a ritualistic Muslim, and certainly not one inclined to side with his coreligionists over the country he felt indebted to. But when my father felt that a part of his identity was under fire, however secondary it might have been in his overall makeup under normal circumstances, that part flared and rose to the surface and began dominating his personality. Bosnia was the straw that broke the camel's back. My father had silently watched the powers that be wreak havoc in the Muslim world for decades: the U.S. support of Iran's despotic shah during the 1970s, the Soviet invasion of Afghanistan at the end of that decade, Israel's military response to the Palestinian uprising in the late 1980s. If such events could anger my Reaganite father, whose religious belief was strong but private, I can understand how the fury of Muslims with deeper ties to the global *ummah* (Muslim community) and less success relating to the West spurred them to action.

Looking back, I see flashes of the ingredients that prepared the ground for Hasib Hussain's suicide mission in my own life: A gut-wrenching feeling of being excluded from mainstream society, in the form of a constant barrage of racist bullying. A vague sense of being Muslim from my mother without any real grounding in how that was relevant or useful to my life. A growing consciousness, through my father, that people with whom I shared an identity were being horribly treated elsewhere, often by people who looked like the ones who were bullying me here.

Like Hasib, I took a step down the path of adolescent risk taking. Unable to find my place in junior high, I started hanging out with kids who pushed their way to the back of the bus, smoked cigarettes across the street from school, stole wine coolers from their parents' refrigerators, and bragged loudly about touching their girlfriends' breasts, while the girls in question giggled within earshot. My mother called them "the boys who ride dirt bikes." My dad made it clear that he didn't want them around. But my parents often didn't get home until 7:00 p.m. or later on weekdays, and so I snuck around with this group as much as I could. Truth be told, I didn't like them much. But as long as I laughed at their crass jokes and brought my collection of heavy metal cassettes to their homes, they seemed amenable to letting me hang around.

Like Hasib, I needed a course correction. My grades were slipping. I was talking back to my parents and coming home with stories glorifying the fights I had seen my friends get into. Perhaps in another place and time, I would have followed a Mohammad Sidique Khan into the back room of an Iqra Learning Center and listened to a man with a regulation-size beard scold me for giving in to adolescent temptations when Muslims across the world were suffering. Maybe I would have sought his discipline and approval and discovered my identity in the imagined community of the global jihad.

How does one ordinary young person's commitment to a religion turn into a suicide mission and another ordinary young person's commitment to that same faith become an organization devoted to pluralism? The answer, I believe, lies in the influences young people have, the programs and people who shape their religious identities.

Religious totalitarians like Sheikh Omar are exceptionally perceptive about the crisis facing second-generation immigrant Muslims in the West. They know that our parents, whose identities were formed in the Middle East, North Africa, and South Asia half a century ago, have a dramatically different set of reference points than we do. They know that the identity we get from them feels irrelevant, that it is impossible to be a 1950s-era Pakistani or Egyptian or Moroccan Muslim in twenty-first-century Chicago or London or Madrid.

In many cases, our parents built bubbles for themselves when they moved to the West—little worlds where they could eat familiar food, speak their own language, and follow the old ways. And because they re-created a little piece of Karachi in Manchester, England, or a part of Bombay in Boston, Massachusetts, they assumed that their children would remain within the cocoon. But we second- and third-generation Muslims cannot separate ourselves from the societies we

THE CROSSROADS OF THE IDENTITY CRISIS

live in. We watch MTV, go to public schools, cross borders that are invisible to our parents dozens of times a day, and quickly understand that the curves of our lives cannot adapt to the straight lines our parents live by. Raised in pious Muslim homes, occasionally participating in the permissive aspects of Western culture, many of us come to believe that our two worlds, the two sides of ourselves, are necessarily antagonistic. This experience of "two-ness" is exacerbated by the deep burn of racism. It is much worse for South Asian Muslims in Britain than it is here in the States. They listen to the prime minister say that they are British, cheer the local sports teams, but still find themselves virtually under siege by gangs of white youths, some wearing the trademark red shoelaces of the National Front, one of several well-organized white racist groups in Britain.

As we grow older and seek a unified Muslim way of being, it is too often Muslim extremists who meet us at the crossroads of our identity crisis. They say, "Look how Muslims are being oppressed all over the world. You, who are living in the belly of the beast and indulging in its excesses, have only one way to purify yourself: to become death and kill."

Where are the Muslim leaders who understand this complex challenge, who are helping young people develop a coherent, relevant Muslim identity in the West? Most Muslim leaders are busy meeting other needs of the community—building mosques and Muslim councils, developing relationships with Western politicians and urban police departments. But most are not involved enough in the lives of young people.

People such as Dr. Umar Abd-Allah, Sheikh Hamza Yusuf, Imam Zaid Shakir, and Professors Sherman Jackson and Amina McCloud in the United States are the exceptions. They understand that the American project and the continuity of Muslim identity are symbiotic, not opposed to each other. They are some of the leading intellectuals in contemporary Islam, and they spend an enormous amount of time running seminars for Muslim college students and retreats for young Muslim leaders. One of their counterparts in Britain, Zaki Badawi (who died in January 2006), spent a lifetime trying to address the challenge of nurturing Muslim identity in the West but knew only too well that the type of leadership he exemplified was all too rare in Britain. When Tony Blair asked him and a group of other senior Muslim leaders why radicals such as Sheikh Omar were so effective with young people, Badawi said, "The young people who believe in him, we do not have access to them." The truth is, not enough Muslim leaders are trying.

A senior leader of the Leeds Muslim community made a similar confession to the *New York Times:* "Why this damage to their own streets, their own cities, their own communities? Maybe if we had paid attention then this wouldn't have happened."

A young Muslim who worked at a corner shop in Leeds expressed the same frustration from his perspective: "The older generations and the younger ones just don't talk like you think they should. Extremists don't walk into mosques and say 'Excuse me, would you like to join me in blowing up London?' It just doesn't work that way." What he meant was that extremists take the time and energy to build strong relationships with young Muslims, while too many members of the established older generation don't even try to connect.

Reading this, I could not help but think of a funeral I had attended for the mother of a twenty-year-old Muslim friend. The death had come as a complete shock. Sohail was sleeping when a neighbor knocked on the door and said that his mother, an active woman in her fifties, was lying on the front lawn. She had had a heart attack while shoveling snow off the driveway. The imam who performed the funeral looked uncomfortable around Sohail, his sister, and the group of grieving young people who had developed a deep affection for their mother. His sermon at the burial consisted of this statement: "This woman was a good Muslim and taught Qur'an and Hadith to her children. You must follow her example and teach Islam to your children." Not a word of comfort about the spiritual meaning of death and the afterlife in Islam. No arm around Sohail's shoulder. No lines of transcendence from Rumi about returning to our source. Only a short, cold command. During the most difficult time in Sohail's life, his religious leader failed him. If Sohail ever had a question about faith, the absolute last person he would seek out is this man.

I was lucky. My free fall was stopped by the YMCA. Since my mother had started working, I had been in afterschool care and summer camp at the B. R. Ryall YMCA in Glen Ellyn, Illinois, the suburb of Chicago where I was raised. Kids who wouldn't talk to me in school befriended me at the Y. We played capture the flag and ultimate Frisbee and made up break dancing routines. One day, when my parents were especially late picking my brother and me up, I decided to walk home. I never stopped to think that I didn't have a key. I was on the roof of my house removing my bedroom window when I heard frantic shouting from the driveway. It was my father and several of the Y staff. They had been driving around Glen Ellyn for the past hour looking for me. There were still people in the woods behind the Y searching to see if I had gotten lost there. My dad was furious. He explained that my impulsiveness had worried and inconvenienced a lot of people. I was a little scared going to camp the next day. But Sheila, one of the camp counselors, rubbed my head and said, "I tired my feet out looking for you, kiddo. Man, I'm glad we found you. You're one of my favorites here, and I don't want anything bad to happen to you." I almost jumped into her arms.

As I grew older, my camp counselors encouraged me to join the Leaders Club, a YMCA group for teenagers that focused on volunteering as a key to leadership development. There are Leaders Clubs at Ys across the country, and every summer one-week camps called Leaders Schools are held in different regions. If Y camp was where I first discovered I could be liked, the Central Region Leaders School is where I first recognized I could create and contribute. People were always asking me to take charge of something. I designed the Wednesday service project we did at a senior citizens center. I played the lead in the end-of-week skit. My name showed up on a regular basis in the daily newsletter. Staff members sought my advice on how to deal with troubled participants. I was asked to give nominating speeches for people running for president of Leaders School and was elected to the council one year myself.

I felt physical pain when the week of Leaders School was over. The confident, creative, contributing somebody that had emerged would have to be folded back in so that I could make it through school without being noticed by the bullies. But the memory of the person I had been that week, the person I could be, remained. My grades rose; I stopped hanging out with the boys who rode dirt bikes.

The YMCA's secret is simple; it stems from a genuine love of young people. The conventional wisdom is that young people are scrambling for their place in the world. The YMCA knows that, deep down, young people need more than just a place. A place is too passive, and because the scheme of things is constantly shifting, it's also too fleeting. It's not a place young people need so much as a *role*, an opportunity to be powerful, a chance to shape their world. And so the YMCA nudges them in the direction of leadership—fourteen-year-olds in charge of ten-year-olds at camp, college students coaching high school basketball teams.

At Leaders School, we sang a song called "Pass It On." It uses the metaphor of fire to speak about the sharing of religious faith. I would sing it around the house for weeks after Leaders School was over. (I once slipped and sang a few lines in front of my high school friends, for which I was tortured mercilessly for months.) In one of the moments when my father was feeling especially righteous about his "Muslim-ness," I overheard him expressing concern to my mother that the YMCA, which was after all the Young Men's *Christian* Association, was teaching us Christian songs. "Do you think they are trying to teach Christianity to our kids?" he asked, the tone of his voice a kind of auditory chest thumping.

"I hope so," my mother responded. "I hope they teach the kids Jewish and Hindu songs, too. That's the kind of Muslims we want our kids to be."

In that offhand reply, overheard when I was a teenager, my mother guessed the arc of my life.

2
Growing Up American, Growing Up Other

Consciousness converges with the child as
a landing tern touches the outspread feet of
its shadow on the sand: precisely, toe hits toe.
ANNIE DILLARD

I grew up with religious rituals. Morning and evening, my family
would gather for prayer, hands cupped to receive blessings, forehead
and nose touching the ground in *sijda*, prayer beads sliding through
our fingers as we chanted, "Ya Allah, Ya Allah" (Oh God, Oh God).

I was raised as an Ismaili Muslim. As soon as I learned how to talk,
my mother started teaching me the six-part Du'a (prayer) that Ismailis
recite once in the morning and twice at night. When my grandmother
on my father's side came to visit from Bombay, she made me sit with
her and learn Ismaili *ginans* (devotional songs) line by line, note for
note. I led the Chicago *jamat* (Ismaili congregation) in prayer before
I knew how to ride a bike.

"Say 'Ya Ali, Ya Muhammad' as you go to sleep. It will protect
you," my mother would tell my little brother and me as she tucked
us in. It was my mother's favorite Ismaili chant, calling on the bless-

ing of both the first Shia Imam (Ali) and the Prophet of Islam (Muhammad).

And then one day my father started leaving for work so early that he no longer joined us for morning prayers. Soon I grew accustomed to the phone ringing around 6:00 p.m., my father calling to tell my mother that he had to entertain clients later than expected, and we should go ahead with dinner and prayers without him. For a while we did. And then we didn't. My mother had started her own upward climb in the professional world. Religious ritual did not so much fade into the background as it got elbowed aside by another faith, a force both glittering and suffocating: American achievement.

One thing stayed. "Say 'Ya Ali, Ya Muhammad' as you go to sleep. It will protect you," my mother still whispered as she tucked us in.

My mother always emphasized that Islam is a diverse religion. Any religion with more than a billion adherents spread across eighty countries and a history going back over a thousand years has to be diverse. We Ismailis are a Muslim community that shares a great deal with our coreligionists, but we also are distinct in some ways. We affirm the basic Muslim *shahada,* the declaration of faith that there is no God but God and that Muhammad is His Prophet. As Shia Muslims, we believe that Muhammad appointed his cousin and son-in-law Ali to lead the community after his death. Ali was known as the first Imam. (This is not to be confused with the lowercase imam, as in the person who leads Muslim prayers.) He had the unique ability to interpret the true meaning and application of the Qur'an in changing times and therefore to guide the Muslim community. The Imam chooses his successor from among his family, ensuring that the Imamat (office of the Imam) remains within the Ahl al-Bayt, or the House of the Prophet. Over the course of history, disputes arose over the appointment of certain Imams, and the Shia split into different communities. The largest Shia community, the Ithna'asharis, believe that their Imam is in hiding. The Ismailis are the only Shia community with a living and present Imam.

The past two Ismaili Imams have been important world figures. Sultan Muhammad Shah, the Imam from 1885 to 1957, was a well-respected Muslim statesman, serving as head of the League of Nations and earning a Nobel Peace Prize nomination. The current Imam, Karim al-Husseini, also known as the Aga Khan, has made his mark by building a highly innovative set of health, education, cultural, and poverty-alleviation institutions working across thirty countries, collectively known as the Aga Khan Development Network.

The Ismaili Imam guides both the spiritual and material life of his followers in a manner similar to how a Sufi sheikh guides his followers. Regarding spirituality, Ismailis have been directed to follow a distinctive prayer practice. We recite a six-part prayer once in the morning and twice in the evening rather than the more common Muslim prayer, called the *salat* or *namaz,* performed five times a day. We have private houses of worship called *jamatkhanas,* days of fasting outside of Ramadan, and our own structures for alms giving. Materially, the Imam has encouraged a segment of Ismailis, traditionally a community of merchants, to seek higher education and settle in the West.

My father was in that group. He moved from Bombay to the American Midwest in the mid-1970s to get his MBA at Notre Dame, acquiring a fanatic devotion to Fighting Irish football in the process. Truth be told, my father did not need the Imam to encourage him to leave India. Rock-and-roll music whetted his appetite, and the all-seeing eye of his mother started to feel suffocating. So he whisked his wife and two baby boys off to South Bend, Indiana, land of gray snow and white Catholics.

After business school, my father landed a job in marketing at the Leo Burnett Company in Chicago, no small achievement for an Indian immigrant in the American Midwest in the late 1970s. We moved a few blocks from the only jamatkhana in Chicago, in the Rogers Park neighborhood, an area where Indians and Pakistanis wore their kurta "pajamas" and smoked their beedies on streets they shared with black-hatted Hasids. My parents enrolled my brother and me in a Montessori school. Every day, my father would leave for work at the crack of dawn, and my mother would drive my brother and me forty-five minutes to school. He would return exhausted, and she would come back with stories of how her children seemed unable to prevent themselves from biting the other students or screaming out loud during naptime.

My mother was a teacher, first by personality and then by profession. A trip with her to the grocery store entailed the endless repetition of multiplication tables and Ismaili prayers. She had graduated from a well-known business school in Bombay and soon discovered that the life of an immigrant housewife in America was less than fulfilling. She began studying for her CPA when I was in first grade, dragging me along to the community colleges where her classes were held. She would plop me down in the vending machine area with a plastic bag full of Triscuits and several hours' worth of math problems.

I was riding bikes with a friend on the day her CPA exam results came in. "What's that noise?" he said. "It sounds like someone screaming your name."

I stopped my bike and listened. "Uh, I gotta go," I told him.

I pedaled furiously on my Schwinn and returned home to find a small group of curious neighbors staring at my mother, who was standing on the steps of our apartment building in her yellow nightgown waving a sheet of paper and shouting, "Eboo, I passed! I passed!"

My mother tried her hand in the corporate world, first at Arthur Andersen and then at the McDonald's Corporation, but she did not fit well into the cubicle life. Her prayers were answered when the College of DuPage announced that it was looking for an accounting professor. She has been in the classroom ever since.

My parents followed the path of successful immigrants, moving out of the city and into an apartment in an inner-ring suburb and then into a large house in Glen Ellyn, a suburb that shouted upward mobility. Our jamatkhana was forty minutes away. My father's new re-

sponsibilities as a vice president at Leo Burnett meant that he was often away on business. The crush of preparing for class, mentoring students, and serving on committees kept my mother overly occupied.
Religious ritual got caught in the squeeze.

That was fine with me. My energy was focused on trying to fit in
as a brown kid in a white world. I would strategize in bed before going
to sleep, asking myself questions such as "What can I do to make the
popular white kids at school accept me, or at least not harass me?" On
the handful of important religious holidays when my parents dragged
my brother and me to jamatkhana, I would look at the sea of brown
people dressed in kurtas and *salwar-kameezes* (Indian tunics), mouth-
ing Arabic prayers with their eyes closed and their bodies swaying,
comically wagging their hands while telling stories in Gujarati, and I
would feel as if they were an inferior breed. I was no longer only wondering what the white kids at school would say about these people. I
had adopted their sneer.

For many years, my closest connection to Islam was my mother's
insistence that I not eat pork. When the fifth grade of Park View Elementary School went on a camping trip, the choice for Friday night
dinner was sausage or pepperoni pizza. My mother complained, insisting that a slice with just cheese be provided for me. When we gathered excitedly to eat, the principal called my name first. "Eboo," he
said, "come get your special piece of pizza." I hung my head and slunk
to the front while the other kids snickered.

When I was invited to a birthday party, my mother would call the
host and make sure that the food being served did not have pork. If
hot dogs were the order of the day, she would hand me a plastic bag
with two beef frankfurters and tell me to remind whoever was cooking to use a separate pan. "But why, Mom?" I would ask plaintively.
"What's the big deal?" I could do nothing about the fact that my skin
color marked me as different, but certainly I could try to be like the
white kids in every other way.

My mother would flare up in anger. "Because we are Muslims. We do not eat pork," she would yell. And then louder: "WE DO NOT EAT PORK." As I did my best to eliminate the last vestiges of tradition, she was desperately trying to hold on to them.

In high school, I had stretches where an inner desire to connect with God gripped me. Some Sundays, my mother would wake up at 3:30 a.m. to go to morning prayers at the jamatkhana, and I started accompanying her. I tested myself by playing basketball while fasting and took pride in refraining from the water and food my friends indulged in afterward. In my mind, this had little to do with Islam. It was more about a deep longing that I could not describe but needed somehow to satisfy. I remember telling my mother stories about a kid in my school I admired, a star athlete and honors student who generally managed to be a nice guy, too. "But he said he doesn't believe in God," I told her. "It makes me think he's missing something."

My mother gave me a look of shock, as if to say, "Somehow, something I've done regarding religion has sunk in." Wisely, she didn't say anything out loud.

"Your great-grandfather moved from a village in Gujarat to the city of Bombay carrying nothing but a can of ghee [clarified butter] and a wristwatch. He sold vegetables off a pushcart for a living, making two paise per item. He baked in the sun and slept by the side of the road."

Sometimes my father would draw the story out even longer. Sometimes my great-grandfather almost starved to death, but pulled through when he thought of the foundation he was laying for his family. Other times all of his wares were washed away in the monsoon, and he had to rebuild his business, vegetable by vegetable. After my father was satisfied that he had made my great-grandfather sound sufficiently heroic and intimidating, he would raise his voice and wave his arms to make his point: "He worked his ass off to get us here. So you have no right to be such a lazy pug."

I heard this lecture on a weekly basis when I was in junior high. My parents had done their best to impress on me that they had sacrificed mightily to settle in Glen Ellyn so my brother and I could attend the best schools. We were unmoved, more focused on being goofballs than getting good grades. My father felt as if he needed to call the ancestors in for reinforcement. I knew that if my dad caught me rolling my eyes at this story, he would be furious. So I cast them downward whenever I saw him wind up to deliver it, and I bit my lip almost until it bled to keep myself from smirking.

My parents had lobbied hard for me to be included in Challenge classes, meant for the cream of the crop at Glen Crest Junior High. My prior academic and behavioral record had been spotty, but my parents badgered the administration until they relented and let me into the program. I didn't hold up my end of the bargain. Even after my phase with the boys who rode dirt bikes had passed, I was still only a so-so student. Class time, in my mind, was best used to try to figure out how to jam an entire pack of Fruit Stripe gum into my mouth. Who needed to learn how to diagram sentences or solve algebra problems?

An offhand comment made by my science teacher, Mr. Schrage, catalyzed a profound change in my life. Schrage ran a special seminar for seventh- and eighth-grade Challenge science students designed to teach us how to do original research. He also happened to be my sixth-grade Challenge science teacher. I believe it was in his class that I finally succeeded in placing all twenty-four sticks of Fruit Stripe gum in my mouth. I raised both hands in a sign of triumph, but I couldn't say much because my mouth was full and turning various shades of blue thanks to the artificial colors in the gum. Perhaps because it was close to the end of the school year, Schrage didn't take the trouble to have me formally removed from the Challenge science program, believing that I would make both of our lives easier and drop down to a regular science course for the rest of my junior high career.

I didn't get the hint. I walked into his class on the first day of seventh grade and made for my typical seat in the back. But before I got there, I heard Schrage say, in utter seriousness, "Didn't we get rid of you last year?"

He said it loud enough for some other students—the type who spent their class time taking notes on Schrage's lectures—to hear.

I could feel them snickering. My neck got hot. I felt tears coming. Schrage, usually a lighthearted jokester, wasn't laughing. He was staring me down. He meant to win this. I had been a thorn in his side the previous year, and he was not about to have me disrupt his class again. All of these things went through my mind at once. I opened my mouth to say something and then closed it. There was nothing to say. Schrage was right.

And then I had another thought: "Does this guy think that I'm not smart enough to write a Challenge science research paper?" Suddenly, I got mad. I prepared to hurl a stream of defiance at him.

But my anger was interrupted by a scarier thought:. "Am I smart enough?" I had never really applied myself to anything. What if I tried this Challenge science research project thing and failed? Schrage would be right. All the other kids in the Challenge program who treated me as if I didn't belong with them would be right. Up until then, I had pretended that I was too cool to do homework or study for exams. So what if my grades weren't as high as everybody else's? My goal was to create the aura that I could do well if I wanted to. I realized that I was the only person in the room who bought that story. And at that moment, I wasn't so sure that I believed myself anymore.

I sat quietly at my desk for that first day of class, keeping my Fruit Stripe gum in my pocket. I didn't cry; that was a victory. But I wanted to, and that was something, too. By virtue of his insult, Schrage helped me discover an identity that was so deeply buried I didn't even know it existed. I wanted to be a good student—no, an *exceptional* student. I wanted to be the kind of student whom other people whispered about when I walked down the hall: "There goes Eboo. That kid is *smart*." I wanted teachers to say, "This was outstanding," when they handed my paper back. I wanted to be asked to read my essay out loud in front of the class.

I returned to Schrage's classroom after the last bell of the day. "I want to be in Challenge science," I told him. "I want to write the best research paper you have ever seen."

Schrage could have told me that the decision to place me in regular science class had already been made by the department head. Sorry. He could have said that I wasn't prepared to write the paper—even if I had an attitude change, I just didn't have the writing or research skills. He could have been brutally honest and said that none of the teachers at Glen Crest had any faith that I would amount to anything, and they didn't like me much anyway. For all they cared, I could sit in the back of the classroom and stick my fingers in my mouth, as long as I didn't bother anybody.

Instead, he took a risk. "Find a topic by next week," he said. I left with a mission.

I chose to write on the topic of chiropractic medicine. There was no good reason why, I just liked the word "chiropractic." I spent nights and weekends buried in the subject. I checked out every book on the topic from the library at the College of DuPage, where my mother taught. I discovered that the National College of Chiropractic was based in the western suburbs of Chicago, and I spent weekends in its library. I learned the different regions of the back, studied the various types of scoliosis, and interviewed local chiropractors about the details of their practice. More important, I learned that I *liked* this research thing. I enjoyed reading several perspectives on a subject and having to juice them into something that was coherent and distinctly my own. I liked tapping my forehead with my pencil trying to get a sentence just right. I liked feeling smart.

My father helped me type the paper the week before it was due. It came in at seventy-two pages. "This might be the longest paper any seventh grader has ever written," he told me, tousling my hair. He was proud of me. I hadn't heard the story about my great-grandfather in weeks. Maybe my father thought that I had absorbed some of the old man's work ethic.

I arrived at school early the day the paper was due and went straight to Schrage's classroom. A part of me wanted to be defiant when I handed it to him and say, "Here—stick this, you jerk. You didn't think I could do it." But this process was about more than the chip on my shoulder. Since signaling my second chance, Schrage had been a full partner in this endeavor, meeting with me every other week to check on my progress. Standing in front of him, my dominant emotion was deep gratitude. "We did it," I told him, and handed him the black binder with my paper inside. He whistled softly, warmly, as he flipped through it, checking the table of contents, scanning the index. "Kid, you are something," he finally said.

He put the binder on his desk. The other binders, the projects done by other students in the Challenge program, were piled near the back of the room. "Why aren't you putting my paper over there?" I asked.

"Because I'm using your paper as the example this year. I'm going to show it to all my other classes and my colleagues in the science department as an illustration of what seventh graders can achieve."

"They're not going to believe that it was really me who wrote it," I said.

Adolescent identities can shift in an instant. I went from being a bad boy to a goofball to a Class A nerd. By the time I was in high school, my life was dominated by suburban fantasies of the future comforts of a fat paycheck. My small group of friends and I were convinced that high school achievement was a perfect indicator of the amount of fame and fortune we would enjoy later. We were obsessed with grades, scores on standardized tests, and academic awards. On Saturday nights, we gathered at the local Taco Bell, imagining our careers, arguing over which one of us was going to get the biggest house, the coolest car, the most chicks. Ariel was going to be on the U.S. Supreme Court. Karthik would be head surgeon at a major hospital. Chris would be a scientist at the National Institutes of Health. I would be a high-flying California lawyer, driving statuesque blondes to Lakers games in my red Mercedes, just like the characters I watched on the television show *L.A. Law*.

Most of our fun came in assaulting one another's dreams. "You got a B on the history test," I would needle Karthik. "You'll never get into Harvard Medical School."

"Screw you," he would reply, embarrassed at being called out in front of everyone. "You can't even do basic geometry."

These discussions quickly degenerated into mom jokes and, finally, pathetic nerd brawls, skinny arms flailing wildly about.

The more meaningless the matter, the more intensely we competed. When school let out at 2:50 p.m., we would race home to watch *Jeopardy!* Whoever got the most right answers would win, with the losers inevitably ganging up to pummel the winner.

We were, in short, nauseating.

I told my parents I wanted to drop out of the YMCA Leaders Club and stop volunteering so I could spend more time focusing on schoolwork. I couldn't stand to think that my friends were getting better grades than I was. And I couldn't believe it when my parents said no. What about my great-grandfather and all the work he had done to lay a foundation so that I had the opportunity to get a great education?

My father was nonplused about having his example shoved back in his face, particularly when he felt as if I was skewing the story for dubious reasons. "Your great-grandfather *always* found time to serve others. He was a deeply devoted Ismaili who was constantly doing volunteer service, even when he barely had enough for himself. This is part of our faith, Eboo."

What? My father had always seemed lukewarm about religion. He had been slow to come to prayers even during the years when we had prayed together as a family, and he seemed positively gleeful to flee jamatkhana whenever we went. Now he was citing faith as a reason for me to stick with my volunteer activities. I asked my mother about it.

"Your father's faith is very strong," she explained. "For him, faith is about service, not rituals. His family in India has been involved in service at every level imaginable. One day you will hear the stories. They will make you proud. Your father is doing his best to carry on that tradition here. He has helped dozens of recent immigrants get their start in this country. Green cards, driver's licenses, loans for new businesses—your father helps them with all of those things. Do you ever wonder about those phone calls we get from people who speak only Urdu or Gujarati? Those are the people we are helping."

And so I spent my Saturday mornings teaching swimming lessons to handicapped people at the YMCA. I spent every afternoon at the Y during the weeks before Halloween and Easter helping to set up the haunted house and the Easter egg hunt. I learned something about the lives of people unlike me. I learned to cheer for somebody other than myself.

Watching my friends and I joust over grades and Jeopardy scores, my father became worried that I was beginning to view learning in purely functional terms. He had been an actor and a filmmaker in India, and learning for him was far more than a path to good grades and a fancy job. One day he marched into my room with an armful of books and said, "It's time to start reading real literature." His plan worked. I put aside the Hardy Boys and Great Brain series and inhaled the stack he left on my bedside table. I read Ken Kesey's One Flew over the Cuckoo's Nest and devised a hundred ways R. P. McMurphy and I could outmaneuver Nurse Ratched. I joined Mack and the boys from John Steinbeck's Cannery Row in their schemes to score bottles of "Old Tennis Shoe" and fix up the Palace Flophouse. I left the princely quarters and wandered out into the world with Siddhartha, wondering how my life would change after I encountered old age, sickness, and death.

In school I joined my classmates in complaining about the books we were assigned in English class, pretending to substitute Cliffs Notes for the real thing. But I secretly loved each one. I remember shutting myself in my room for the entire four days of my Thanksgiving vacation during junior year, immersed in Thoreau's Walden. Summers, when I wasn't playing basketball or working at my parent's Subway sandwich shop, were spent rereading my favorite books from the school year—Harper Lee's To Kill a Mockingbird, Ray Bradbury's Dandelion Wine, and Mark Twain's The Adventures of Huckleberry Finn.

I harbored a deep frustration that discussions of books lasted only until the bell rang and were limited to essay assignments and test questions. I remember a mechanical back-and-forth in my high school English class over whether Thoreau had been justified in going to jail to protest the Mexican-American War. The year before (1991), America had invaded Iraq. The people lazily arguing Thoreau's side, including the teacher, did not connect the two. In fact, hardly anybody in my school voiced concern about that war, and certainly nobody suggested we take Thoreau's idea seriously and protest by going to prison. But suddenly I was embarrassed that I had unthinkingly worn a shirt that said SADDAMNED to school during the war. I wasn't clear about whether I thought the invasion was right or wrong, but I had become acutely aware that I had never even asked the question. I looked at "Civil Disobedience" in a different way, and it in turn shed new light on the world around me.

That was the beginning of a broader shift in my thinking. In my head, I loved ideas. In my gut, I knew they counted only when they were connected to reality.

Lisa was different. You could tell just by looking at her. She didn't join the other girls, who gathered in giggling clumps in the hallway, and she didn't seem lonely walking alone. She was quiet in class, but you could tell she wasn't shy. Every once in a while, she would answer a question, and then it was obvious that she had a unique intellect.

Lisa's family moved to Glen Ellyn sometime during my sophomore year. Generally, there was a buzz about any new girl in the boys' locker room, but Lisa did not wear the type of clothes or flash the kind of smile that attracted such attention. She went unnoticed for several weeks. It was my friend Ariel who first mentioned her in our group. It was a Friday night, and we were completing our usual routine of basketball at the YMCA and 59-cent bean burritos at Taco Bell. The conversation turned from taunts about athletic skills to comparative class rank. Karthik wagered that he was in the top five, rattling off his closest competitors and outlining a strategy to overtake them.

"You're forgetting about Lisa," Ariel said.

"Who's that?" he asked, perturbed.

"She's smart," Ariel responded. "She's smarter than you. I think she's smarter than me." Which meant that he was in love with her.

I wish I could say that our courtship was romantic, or at least deliberate. But I was devoid of all sophistication in such areas. For all I know, Lisa was working her designs on me. But however it happened, I was suddenly skipping out of afterschool Jeopardy battles with my friends and instead giving Lisa a ride home every day.

I was a little embarrassed about my car, a 1973 Oldsmobile Cutlass, on which I had spent my life savings of $400. My dad called it "the Cuban canoe." Green paint and brown rust warred to lay claim to the exterior. The driver's side window closed only partway, which meant it was freezing in the winter. The front seat was all one, separated only by a squeaky armrest. My tape deck had gotten stuck with the Who's *Quadrophenia* lodged inside. Sometimes it wouldn't turn off, which meant that "The Real Me" rang loudly in our ears the whole ride home. Lisa never said a word about it. She would slip in on the passenger's side, place her books at her feet, click on her seat belt, and say, "I'm ready."

I prayed that we hit both red lights between Glenbard South High School and her home a mile and a half away. That meant that our conversation about Dante's *Divine Comedy*, which we were reading in advanced placement English, or the film we had seen in our Contemporary American History class could last an extra ninety seconds.

"Look if you like, but you will have to leap," W. H. Auden wrote. And one day I did.

There was no pacing in my room and practicing in front of the mirror, no eternal deliberation or consultation with close friends, no sense of momentous decision, just a blurting out. After Lisa had placed her bag at her feet and before she clicked on her seat belt, I said, "I think it is time that maybe we were more than friends. Do you?"

She looked at me. Then she looked at the ground. Then she looked back at me. "Yes," she said. "No," she said. "Maybe," she concluded.

She reached for her seat belt and then stopped. She lifted the arm-rest that separated the passenger's side from the driver's side, slowly scooted over, and sat quietly next to me. "I'm ready," she said.

We caught both red lights that day, but we didn't do much talking. We were together. Each of us had leaped, leaving one world for another.

I was ready to leave my world of Jeopardy battles and Taco Bell arguments. Lisa was not the type of girl who wanted to hang around and watch my friends and me play basketball and brag to each other. And I was tired of all that anyway.

But Lisa's hesitation in the car belied a much more complex and challenging issue. Lisa was a Mormon. She believed that God had given Joseph Smith revelation, that Mormons were the chosen people, and that America was the promised land. She had dreamed about meeting a husband in church or at Brigham Young University, perhaps a returned missionary who spoke multiple languages, had converted half a dozen families, and had developed a love for the literature of the country where he had been stationed along the way. They would go to PG-rated movies together and drink milk shakes afterward (never coffee or tea; caffeinated beverages were forbidden). They would be married in a Mormon temple and have six children.

Sometimes the family would all sit together in church on Sunday morning; other times the kids would sit separately, giving Lisa and her husband spiritual couple time. Their home would be a magnet for the neighborhood kids, dozens of them gathering to play board games indoors or capture the flag in the neighboring woods. Lisa would bake for them. Her husband would run a business, have the priesthood (meaning he was a male in good standing in the Mormon church), serve with distinction as the bishop of the local ward (meaning he was in a position of leadership among the Mormons in a certain geographical area). Their kids would be adventurous and mischievous, but correctable. If they were caught sneaking soda pop, looking at girlie magazines, or swearing with their friends, they would gently be told that Mormons don't do that, and then they would stop.

When the kids grew up, Lisa would take a job teaching literature at the local college. She would have been writing this whole while, mostly essays for magazines like *Ladies' Home Journal*, but now she would focus more seriously on short stories and poetry. Her family would scrape by but be happy. Perhaps they would live abroad for a few years, serving as advisers to young missionaries. When old age came, they would welcome the crossing into the next world, where their temple wedding would ensure that they would all eventually be re-united forever.

Instead, she met me, an overly long, too-skinny, Indian Muslim who cussed frequently, enjoyed R-rated movies, and was acquiring a taste for coffee.

The battle between my Muslim upbringing and my male hor-mones was resolved by Lisa's Mormon values. One evening, when Lisa and I were sitting close to each other in my basement, she sighed and said she had to do something. She took out a piece of paper and a pen-cil and drew a stick figure. "That's me," she said. And then she care-fully drew a circle over the body, leaving her neck and face, her hands and arms up to the shoulders, and her legs from the knees down out-side the lines. "Inside is out-of-bounds," she told me.

As that aspect of our relationship was limited, we spent our time on other things. I finally had someone to share my secret life of read-ing with. Lisa and I spent summer days at the park, reading to each other from our favorite books. If we saw a late-afternoon movie, we would spend dinner comparing the characters in the film to those in the books we were reading. Her poetic imagination made connections between literature and life that I never saw.

First love is infinite in its variety but singular in its effect. Whether it is a religion, a drug, a book, or a person you fall for, you can expect to emerge on the other side nothing less than totally transformed. And so it was for me with Lisa. My life until that point had been dom-inated by an obsession with my own success. And yet, as I watched Lisa excel in class after class, club after club, her intellect and charac-ter so clearly superior to mine, I found my heart, in spite of myself, rooting for her. Nobody was more surprised at this than I was. Prior to Lisa, I had thought I was capable of only competitiveness. But with Lisa, perhaps because of Lisa, I discovered vast regions within me. It was as good a preparation for my future recommitment to Islam as anything else.

Lisa's religiosity focused on truth. Basically, Mormons had it and others didn't. It was not Lisa's choice that it was this way. She did not control truth; that was God's to give. Did she believe it? Did she follow it? Those were the relevant questions. I could tell it pained her sometimes. My grandmother, my mother's mother, lived with my family while I was in high school. She was as sweet as they come, joyful and pious, cackling loudly at all sorts of jokes when she wasn't praying her tasbih, sneaking pinches of chewing tobacco when my mother wasn't looking (it helped her stay awake, she insisted), and joining my brother and me in clearing the driveway of autumn leaves with the household tool that fit her hand best: a spatula.

"Will she not go to heaven?" I asked Lisa, a bit defiantly, one afternoon.

Lisa turned away. She was too smart not to have asked herself the question, but she couldn't bear the answer. "She will go somewhere good," she finally said. Lisa's answer satisfied me. I could tell it said more about her heart than Mormon theology. I decided her heart mattered more, a conviction that has shaped my life and work ever since. I have been close to many Mormons over the past decade, and I still don't know how Mormon theology regards true believers of other faiths. That moment with Lisa taught me a lasting lesson about the sociology of religion: the heart of even the most ardent religious believer will provide more accurate clues to his or her behavior than the theology of his or her faith.

In a relationship that lasted just over a year, she never made me or my family feel inferior because we were not Mormon. Although I knew she wanted nothing more than for me to convert, she was never condescending or inappropriate in her approach. She mentioned a few times that I could go to church with her, and she gave me a copy of the Book of Mormon, but the discussion never went much beyond that. She let the occasional swear word pass without rebuke and even agreed to see a couple of R-rated movies (although she made me fast-forward through all the "good" parts of *Frankie and Johnny* with Al Pacino and Michelle Pfeiffer). But I knew that a future with Lisa required conversion. I told Lisa that I was reading the Book of Mormon and that I was going to skip basketball with my friends one Sunday morning and join her at church, but I never did. I was in love with a Mormon, but I was agnostic about Mormonism. In fact, I was agnostic about a lot of things by the spring of my senior year in high school. I felt that Glen Ellyn was a town full of walls and those walls were closing in on me. I was ready for a new world.

I cried like a baby the night before Lisa left for Brigham Young University and swore that our long-distance relationship would make it through college. I bought a hundred dollars in phone cards and even explored academic programs at Brigham Young. But when I arrived at the University of Illinois, I felt like my lungs had expanded overnight. Champaign-Urbana was less than a three-hour drive from my home, but the air felt different.

The more I immersed myself in that world, the more I realized that it was my natural habitat. Every interesting film I saw seemed to be rated R, and upon leaving the theater I couldn't help but think, "I couldn't have seen that if I was with Lisa." The books I was most fascinated by were critical of America. I tried talking about it with Lisa, only to be reminded that, for Mormons, America is the land of milk and honey.

Lisa came with another world, and at Brigham Young, she was becoming more immersed in it. I could no longer lie to myself or to Lisa. I did not know what direction I was going in, but I knew I had to let my lungs expand. Lisa began asking more frequently whether I was reading the Book of Mormon, and I stopped lying to her. I cried like a baby, again, when Lisa told me that she needed to move on. But I knew that we both already had.

3

Identity Politics

All creatures come into the world
bringing with them the memory of justice.

J. M. COETZEE

My first college memory is at the gym. There are three basketball games going on—a black game, an Asian game, and a white game. I am confused, but not about who I am. I know I am white. I have spent years making myself so. That is why I started playing basketball in the first place. It is what the popular white kids at my school did. I figured the physical defect of my brown skin would be overlooked if I perfected a fifteen-foot jump shot. The basketball court, to my eyes, was a big bucket of skin whitener.

I looked at the black and Asian kids. They seemed so comfortable. They shouted at one another up and down the court in a distinct flow, ran pick-and-rolls and give-and-gos in their own unique rhythms. Didn't they want to play on the white court? Hadn't they spent years studying the white game so they could make its moves their own? Isn't that what it means to be colored in America?

The world has never seemed so new to me as it did during those first few months of college. My first lesson was on race. I was stunned

37

to learn that not everybody wanted to be white. I remember seeing a Korean girl I had gone to high school with across the hall at the Illini Union. "Kristen," I called out. But she didn't turn around. "She went back to her Korean name," a mutual friend, also Korean, later explained when I told her about the incident. "She won't answer to Kristen anymore."

"What the hell is that about?" I asked.

"It happens to a lot of Koreans when they go to college. They become more involved in their own ethnicity and culture. They hang out only with other Koreans."

She was using college as a place to de-whiten herself. The more I looked around, the more I realized that she wasn't the only one. Cafeterias were balkanized by race and ethnicity. Unlike in high school, where the popular (mostly white) kids sat at one table and others longed for a place there, people wanted to be where they were. In fact, they were fiercely proud and protective of their own zones.

Every residence hall, in addition to having a general student council, had a black student union. I had a class with the president of the black student union at Allen Hall, where I lived during my freshman and sophomore years, and was impressed by his intellect and passion. "Why don't you run for president of Allen Hall Council?" I asked. "I think you'd be great. I think you'd get elected."

"Fuck Allen Hall Council," he responded. "Everything I do, I do for black people." The black kid sitting next to him didn't even turn to face us. He just nodded.

I remember the moment that this made sense to me. During the first semester of college, I found myself entranced by a beautiful young woman in my geology class. It goes without saying that she was white; that was the definition of beauty to me. Class after class, I looked for my opening, and one day I got close enough to flash a direct smile at her and approach. She shot me a look of disgust, turned around, and began walking the other way with a group of equally beautiful, equally white girls.

I remember thinking, "Well, I shouldn't have tried anyway. Girls like that don't go for guys like me." And then I stopped in my tracks. What did I mean by that? Basically this: pretty white girls don't go for brown guys. My skin color, my ethnic name, the food my mother cooked meant no access to certain circles. I had learned that rule at a very young age and lived by it for many years. Violating that invisible code risked the punishment of ridicule.

For so long, I had simply accepted this as a fact of life. But college gave me a different framework in which to see race. The problem was not with my skin; it was with her eyes.

Having swallowed the pill of white supremacy whole during high school and allowed its poison to spread through my body, I suppose it should have come as no surprise that I would accept uncritically the first elixir that presented itself. That elixir was identity politics, and it was in full swing during my undergraduate years.

The grand idea of identity politics circa 1994, or at least the way my crew and I understood it, was this: the world, and one's place in it, was entirely defined by the color of one's skin, the income of one's parents, and the shape of one's genitalia. Middle-class white men had built a culture, an economy, and a political system designed to maintain their own power. First they called it Western civilization, then they called it America, and now they were calling it globalization. These people were the oppressors. The rest of us, the oppressed, had been pawns in their game for far too long. A few heroes over time had picked up on this, and the bravest among them—Nat Turner, Lucy Parsons, Stokely Carmichael—had revolted. The rise of identity politics was the beginning of a new age, a great intellectual liberating force that allowed us not only to understand the true workings of the system but also to perceive and return to our own authentic selves.

Our authentic selves were, of course, totally determined by our ascribed race, class, and gender identities, which shaped everything from one's politics to one's friendships to one's tastes in food and music. To be black was to be liberal, at least; if you knew anything about your history (which, to us, meant a brush with Marcus Garvey or Frederick Douglass), you were awakened to your true political nature,

which was to be radical. A black Republican? No such thing. What of
Colin Powell and Clarence Thomas? We had two explanations: they
had been duped by the white power structure (and therefore weren't
really Republicans), or they were willing to sell out their own people
for personal profit (and therefore weren't really black).

We spent countless hours discussing nomenclature: black or African American, Hispanic or Latino, Native American or Indigenous
Person? We argued to the point of blows over the nature of various oppressions. Were black women more oppressed based on their race or
their gender? Who was more marginalized, African Americans, Latinos, or Native Americans? The Asian Americans, feeling a bit left
out, invited a radical Asian American speaker to campus who gave a
talk called "Where Are the Asian American Malcolm Xs"?

"The personal is political" was our battle cry. Selective individual
actions were immediately refracted into large-scale truths. It wasn't
just four white cops who beat Rodney King; it was every white person
oppressing every person of color on earth.

In high school history class, America had been presented as the
land of opportunity and freedom. I had been told almost nothing
about its dark side. But now I couldn't get enough. I read Howard
Zinn's account of Columbus's voyage and was sickened that the man
we celebrate as "discovering" America made plans to exploit the indigenous people here as soon as he laid eyes on them. I learned that
the Gulf of Tonkin Resolution, which led to a massive escalation
of the Vietnam War, was probably based on a lie. President Lyndon
Johnson had sent waves of poor and minority Americans to destroy a
country because of his ego. Power will always oppress people, one of
my professors said.

The evidence for that was right in front of me. Champaign-
Urbana wasn't much of a city, but it had many more social problems
than Glen Ellyn. All you had to do was open your eyes to see Vietnam
vets on the street drinking mouthwash for the alcohol and black kids
in the poor part of town going to schools far inferior to the tony University High where the professors sent their children.

I began to see the world through the framework of my radicalizing political consciousness. As I watched drunk white frat boys mock homeless people on Green Street on Friday nights, I saw corporate fat cats eating caviar while poor Americans starved during the Great Depression. When the crowds of Fighting Illini fans streamed by on their way to a basketball game wearing T-shirts and hats displaying the university's demeaning mascot, Chief Illiniwek, I saw the spirit of Christopher Columbus crushing the natives.

My response was to rage. I remember shouting down my fellow students in sociology classes at the University of Illinois for suggesting that welfare should be reformed so that poor people took more personal responsibility, angrily protesting against conservative speakers who came to campus, calling anybody who applied for a corporate job a sellout. "America is bent on imperialism" was the first thought I had every morning and the last thought I had every night.

I was guided mostly by 1960s-era radical black thought—H. Rap Brown, Huey Newton, early Malcolm X. The key lesson I took from this material was that progress was a myth. It was revolution or nothing. I quoted Malcolm X to the mealy-mouthed liberals who cited the victories of the civil rights movement: "You can't stick a knife into a man's back nine inches, pull it out six inches, and call that progress." I found myself increasingly enamored of the occasional references to the value of violence. "Every time a cop murders somebody in Harlem" I read in one volume, "we will retaliate by murdering someone in midtown." "By any means necessary" was Malcolm X's famous line. It made infinite sense to me. If the American system's primary tool of engagement was violence, then those of us who sought to change it would have to become fluent in that language.

I found myself pushing the envelope more. I started calling liberals "house niggers" a term I learned from reading Malcolm X, meaning they were too domesticated and comfortable to take the necessary actions to bring down the system. My father, growing increasingly frustrated by my stridency, told me to stop talking about politics when I visited home. "You're too bourgeois to see what's really happening in this world," I responded. He exploded in anger, saying something about how his "bourgeois" ways were paying my college tuition. I took his anger as evidence that I was on the right path. Every radical had been rejected, even mocked, when he first spoke truth to power. My father's frustration was confirmation that I had gained entry into the tradition of righteous revolutionaries.

I searched for models of people who had tried to block the machinery of American imperialism. One of the campus radicals said to me, "Have you ever heard of Bill Ayers and Bernardine Dohrn? They started an outfit in the 1960s called the Weather Underground that did strategic bombing here in the U.S. You should check them out."

I filed that away in the back of my head. I was sure the reference would come in handy someday.

Gone were my high school dreams of a perfect LSAT score and a prime corporate law job in LA. I had liberated myself from the capitalist framework that provides comfort for some and poverty for most. I had left the known world and entered the universe of myth.

The one thing that connected me to my past was volunteering. Something about my YMCA experiences and my parents' insistence that service was essential stuck with me. Also, I needed the human connection. My head was swimming with radical theories and my spirit was bursting with anger. The moments I spent trying to concretely improve somebody's life kept me from falling over the edge. Every Sunday morning, I went to a nursing home and played my guitar for the residents. On alternate Monday nights, I helped cook dinner and clean the kitchen at the women's shelter. Thursdays I picked up cakes and cookies from a local bakery and delivered them to the Salvation Army. The leaders of local social service agencies became some of my closest mentors in Champaign.

But my intellectual and activist friends were cool toward such activities. They thought that social services were part of the "system" and that by volunteering I was helping perpetuate the injustices inherent in capitalism. The litmus test they used for any initiative was

whether it was "radical," by which they meant, will this activity ultimately destroy the current system? I stopped telling them about the
new programs I had started as president of the Allen Hall Volunteer
Group because they would inevitably dismiss them with a wave of
a clove cigarette and a single line: "That sounds like just another
middle-class liberal program."

No doubt there was something superficial about a good deal of
the volunteering that took place when I was a student. The other students I worked with at homeless shelters and tutoring programs took
their volunteer activities seriously, but when I tried to start discussions
on the causes of homelessness or educational inequality, they didn't
want to hear it. "Volunteering at the Salvation Army for two hours on
Thursday night makes me feel like I am giving back," one of them told
me. "Then I don't feel bad when I go out and have fun on Friday night."

"Yeah, but those guys you play cards with on Thursday night are
still at the Salvation Army on Friday while you are out partying," I
thought. If the primary purpose of volunteering is to help other people, not to assuage our own guilt, shouldn't we spend some time thinking about how to improve the situation of homeless people in a more
permanent way?

But I was also aware of a more creative movement bubbling up. It
had volunteering at its core, but its broader mission was social change.
Organizations such as Teach for America, City Year, and Habitat
for Humanity combined the concrete activities of typical volunteer
programs with an exciting vision of large-scale transformation. If you
volunteered with a Habitat for Humanity project, you weren't just
building houses; you were ending poverty housing. If you joined Teach
for America, you weren't just helping 30 fourth graders; you were
transforming American education. At City Year, you weren't just doing jumping jacks in the park wearing a bright red jacket; you were
showing the world that young people were idealistic change makers,
not self-absorbed cynics.

Moreover, these organizations took diversity seriously. They realized that service was an ideal place to bring together people from dif-

ferent racial, ethnic, class, and geographic backgrounds. People built a special relationship with one another when they passed bricks at a Habitat for Humanity site or planned lessons for children at an inner-city school. The common purpose gave them a common bond. Furthermore, because these people came from different backgrounds, they inevitably brought different perspectives to the various challenges that emerged in their service projects. In other words, a diverse team made for better service.

As my angry activist friends bemoaned the lack of participation in our political meetings, I watched thousands of people, from economics majors to English majors, flock to Teach for America, Habitat for Humanity, and City Year. These organizations had managed to create an aura around themselves. They were far larger than the particular programs; they had become ideas in the culture. President Bill Clinton recognized this and created AmeriCorps to build on that energy. The *New York Times* and other major publications took notice and wrote articles extolling these groups. I realized that Wendy Kopp of Teach for America, Vanessa Kirsch of Public Allies, and Alan Khazei and Michael Brown of City Year were not much older than I was. They had founded their organizations when they were recent college graduates. I had been made to believe that our only heroes were martyrs of the 1960s. I was proud to know that my generation had produced leaders, too.

The dorm I lived in, Allen Hall, was a temple of radical politics and cultural creativity. It was the University of Illinois's first Living-Learning Community, meaning that academic courses were offered in the dorm itself, with the intention of cultivating a liberal arts college–type intellectual atmosphere. "Freaks and geeks" was what the rest of the campus called it.

One of the first people I met at Allen Hall was a tall, lanky senior named Jeff Pinzino. He embodied Allen Hall perfectly. When I came back from class in the afternoon, he was inevitably on the porch, playing Hacky Sack and harmonica with the hippie types. He was into

things like ethnomusicology and Alan Watts, and had organized theater troupes, writing groups, and political discussion circles in the hall.
Jeff had an almost perfect grade point average, but nobody had ever
seen him study. The only time I ever saw him in the library, he was listening to Delta blues musicians in the music archive. I once saw him
reading a brochure for the Maharishi University in Iowa. When I
asked him about it, he told me it was one of the graduate programs he
was considering, along with Stanford and the University of Chicago.

I loved Jeff's offbeat interests, but even more I loved his ability to
make things happen. "Why do you spend so much time starting little
groups?" I once asked him.

"Because the most important thing you can learn is how to turn an
idea into reality," he responded. I wrote that phrase down in my journal and underlined it three times.

The director of Allen Hall, Howie Schein, was an aging hippie
who had received his PhD from Berkeley during its political heyday.
Committed to social justice and student empowerment in his own
low-key way, Howie attracted the campus's most politically radical
and student-centered faculty to teach courses at Allen. Allen's section
of Introduction to Political Science was famously taught by a Marxist
who had played a prominent role in the organization of Vietnam Vet-
erans Against the War. Howie also had music rooms and art studios
built in the hall, found funding for students to create political and cultural programs, and started one of the nation's first guest in residence
programs, which brought writers, artists, and political agitators to live
in the hall and interact with students for one to two weeks. The purpose, he once told me, was to show students that accounting, law, engineering, and medicine were not the only life paths available.

It was a guest in residence at Allen Hall who nudged me toward
my second serious relationship. Emily Shihadeh, a Palestinian American playwright, performed her one-woman play about growing up in
Ramallah and inventing her own destiny in San Francisco to a rapt
audience at Allen Hall. I loved her. She had my mother's strength of
will and my father's sense of humor. She wanted to see Champaign, so

I took her to all the places I volunteered: the nursing home where I played music, the homeless shelter where I served dinner, the elementary school where I taught peace games to children. Driving back to Allen Hall after one of these excursions, she turned to me and said, "I can see what you are doing. You are trying to give all of your love away through these different service activities. It is good you are helping people, but you will never get full from it. This kind of love you have has to be given to one person, a special person."

I told her about Sarah. We had met at a student leadership conference and been friends ever since. The activist circle at Illinois was small, so we ran into each other a lot. Earlier that year, we had founded a program that took residents of one of the homeless shelters for social outings once a week. We were often the only two students who showed up, and after we took the residents back to the shelter, we would go to Zorbas for a sandwich and some late-night blues. One night, after we dropped the guys off, Sarah looked up at the sky and said, "Tonight is a perfect night for star spinning."

"What's that?" I asked.

"You've never been star spinning?" she asked in mock surprise. And so we drove to a field a few miles from campus, crossed our wrists, grabbed each other's hands, and spun around looking skyward. We fell down, arms sprawled out, laughing hysterically.

If I hadn't felt so dizzy, I might have reached for her, I told Emily. "Oh, *habibi*," she said to me, using an Arabic term of affection. "You go to this beautiful girl before she concludes you are too stupid and looks for someone else."

Being Jewish was central to Sarah's identity. She had been raised in Jewish youth programs; had twice been on the March of the Living, where young Jews visit the sites of concentration camps in Europe; and had served on the international board of B'nai B'rith's youth organization. When we met, she was studying Hebrew in preparation for a semester in Israel.

Whereas Lisa's religiosity was based on notions of truth, Sarah's was based on commitment to peoplehood and social justice. She did not strictly keep Shabbat, the Jewish day of rest, but she lit candles every Friday evening in honor of its arrival. "My great-grandmother lit candles, my grandmother lit candles, my mother lights candles, so I will light candles," she explained to me. Her parents had escaped Romania's brutal dictator Ceausescu in the early 1970s and moved to Israel. They had left Israel for the United States, then returned when war broke out in 1973. Sarah would joke, "Most people leave countries when wars happen. My parents moved back." But I understood the seriousness behind what she was saying. Her people had been willing to fight for Jewishness, and Sarah felt it was her honor and responsibility to be a part of the tradition and community that others had fought and died for.

Sarah spoke often about *tikkun olam* and *tzedakah*, the Hebrew terms for repairing the world and doing charity. These were the most important principles of Judaism to her, and in her eyes they commanded Jews to help all humanity, especially those who are suffering. I remember going with Sarah to Foellinger Auditorium at the University of Illinois to hear a Holocaust survivor speak about his experiences. Sarah wept throughout the talk. She had visited the concentration camp this man had been in. When the speech was done, Sarah asked the first question: "I have been involved in Holocaust education since I was twelve. I lived by the motto 'Never again.' But it *is* happening again, now, before our eyes, in Bosnia. What will make it stop?"

A hush fell over the audience. The man onstage mumbled something weak, congratulating Sarah for caring. The Q and A continued, but Sarah's question hung in the room for the remainder of the event. She and I left. I was quieter than usual. "What's wrong?" she asked.

"Nothing really," I told her. "It's just that the only other person I've heard talk about what's happening in Bosnia is my dad. He's so angry that it's Muslims being massacred there. He's convinced that if it was Christians or Jews, the rest of the world would try to stop it."

"I just think it's horrible, all those people being killed," Sarah said. "I didn't even know they were Muslims. But whoever they are, the world should come to their aid."

Something occurred to me. In all the sociology courses on identity I had taken, in all the late-night conversations we had at Allen Hall on the subject, the issue of religion rarely came up. We were always talking about freedom for women or Latinos or lesbians. Identity was always defined as race, class, gender, or, occasionally, sexual orientation. When I became a resident adviser, half of my training focused on dealing with issues around those particular identities. The service learning movement took diversity seriously, but it was always about blacks and whites, poor folks and rich folks, urbanites and suburbanites; never about Muslims, Christians, and Jews. I had been to many programs at the Office of Minority Student Affairs, and they also had always focused on the same things. We talked about the limited roles for black actors, the discrimination that kept gay politicians in the closet, the burden of the second shift for women, the cultural capital that accrued to middle-class kids because of the circumstances of their birth. We extolled bell hooks and Gloria Anzaldua for their ability to write about these various identities in an integrated way, and filled hours debating whether the oppressions associated with each identity *added* together or *multiplied* together. But right now, as we griped about Denzel Washington getting passed over for the Oscar for *Malcolm X*, a religious war was raging in the Balkans, tens of thousands of people were dying, and *faith was nowhere to be found in the diversity discussion*.

What I didn't tell Sarah at that time, what I had told few people actually because I didn't know how to make sense of it myself, was that I had recently discovered religion.

I had come across a copy of Robert Coles's *The Call of Service* and was drawn to one of the people he wrote about: Dorothy Day. He spoke of her with absolute awe, as if she was a force of nature. In her thirties, during the Great Depression, Day had started something called the Catholic Worker movement, which combined radical politics, direct service, and community living. For nearly half a century, Day had given up her own middle-class privilege to live with those who went without in what was called a Catholic Worker House of Hospitality. The original House of Hospitality was on the Lower East Side of New York City, but it inspired more than a hundred others across the nation.

Like everything else that seemed good, I was convinced that the Catholic Worker movement had faded away in the 1960s.

"Oh, no," somebody told me when I made an offhand reference to the Catholic Worker and bemoaned its disappearance. "There are still many, many Catholic Worker houses left. In fact, there is one here in Champaign."

"What's it like?" I asked, shocked.

"Part shelter for poor folks, part anarchist movement for Catholic radicals, part community for anyone who enters. Really, it's about a whole new way of living. You've got to go there to know."

From the moment I entered St. Jude's, it was clear to me that this was different from any other place I'd been. I couldn't figure out whether it was a shelter or a home. There was nobody doing intake. There was no executive director's office. White, black, and brown kids played together in the living room. I smelled food and heard English and Spanish voices coming from the kitchen. The first thing somebody said to me was, "Are you staying for dinner?"

"Yes," I said.

The salad and stew were simple and filling, and the conversation came easy. After dinner, I asked someone, "Who are the staff here? And who are the residents?"

"That's not the best way to think about this place," the person told me. "We're a community. The question we ask is, 'What's your story?' There is a family here who emigrated from a small village in Mexico. The father found out about this place from his Catholic parish. They've been here for four months, enough time for the father to find a job and scrape together the security deposit on an apartment. There are others here with graduate degrees who believe that sharing their lives with the needy is their Christian calling. If you want to know the philosophy behind all of this, read Dorothy Day."

I found some of Day's old essays and a copy of her autobiography. In those writings, I found an articulation of what it meant to be human, to be radical, and to be useful. Recalling the thoughts of her college days, Day wrote, "I did not see anyone taking off his coat and giving it to the poor. I didn't see anyone having a banquet and calling in the lame, the halt and the blind. And those who were doing it, like the Salvation Army, did not appeal to me. I wanted life and I wanted the abundant life. I wanted it for others too."

Elsewhere in her autobiography, she wrote: "Why was so much done in remedying social evils instead of avoiding them in the first place? ... Where were the saints to try to change the social order, not just to minister to the slaves but to do away with slavery?"

Here was what I had been seeking for so long: a vision of radical equality—all human beings living the abundant life—that could be achieved through both a direct service approach and a change-the-system politics. For so long, those two things had existed in separate rooms in my life—a different group of friends, a different way of talking for each. Here was a movement that combined them. Finally, the two sides of myself could be in the same room.

The most radical part about Dorothy Day and the Catholic Worker movement was the insistence that everything the movement did was guided by a single force: love. "We have all known the long loneliness and we have learned that the only solution is love and that love comes with community," Day wrote at the end of her autobiography. I felt as if she was talking to me one-on-one. I was tired of raging. It left me feeling empty, and what did it achieve anyway? I wanted to improve people's lives because I loved humanity, not because I hated the system. Sometimes, I thought, my activist friends hated the system more than they loved humanity.

The Catholic Worker became my community. I started making weekly visits to St. Jude House while I was in Champaign. And the summer after my sophomore year, Jeff Pinzino and I did a seven-week road trip through Catholic Worker houses ranging from the Northeast to the Deep South. I cut up carrots for the soup kitchen at St. Joseph's House in New York City; demonstrated at the Pentagon with Catholic Workers in Washington, D.C.; heard the inspiring story of a Vietnam veteran in Atlanta who had climbed back from addiction and mental illness and was now helping others do the same.

More than anything, I marveled at the spirit with which Catholic Workers carried out their tasks. The only word to describe it is grace. I was accustomed to seeing the staff at social service agencies get frustrated, even angry, with the people they were working with (whom they referred to, strangely, as "clients"). I never saw that at a Catholic Worker house. The Houses of Hospitality were, by and large, cultures of kindness. And unlike most of the other demonstrations I went to, which were dominated by anger and self-righteousness, speakers at Catholic Worker demonstrations spoke even their most radical statements with an air of humility and love. When I demonstrated at the Pentagon with a group of Catholic Workers, they didn't shout about how evil soldiers were; they sang hymns and said they would pray for the military brass walking in. Even when Dorothy Day referred to America as a "filthy, rotten system," she somehow managed to do it in a way that called for hopeful, loving change, not anger and rage.

I was intoxicated by Day's vision and felt deep admiration for the Catholic Workers I met. I found myself asking constantly, "What is the source of the love you so often speak of?" Their answer came in one three-letter word that I had rarely heard during my time in college: God.

In *The Call of Service*, Robert Coles described a conversation between one of his Harvard undergraduates and Day in the late 1970s. The young man, a science major, told Day, "You've done so much already for these people."

"The Lord has done it all; we try to be adequate instruments of His," she answered.

"Well, it's been *you folks* who have done all this," the young man insisted, pointing to the soup kitchen in which Day and other Catholic Workers were busily preparing a meal, skeptical of calling in a supernatural power for what seemed clearly to be a human action.

Day was gentle but equally insistent that God was the source of her work. "Oh, when we pray, we are told—we are given answers to our questions. They [the answers] come to us, and then we know He has sent us the thoughts, the ideas. They all don't just belong to us. He lives in our thoughts, the Lord does."

According to Day, all we humans can do is be grateful for the opportunity to hear God's call and ask for the strength to answer it. For Day, that answer came in the form of prayer and work, which to her amounted to much the same thing:

I may be old and near the end, but in my mind, I'm the same old Dorothy trying to show the good Lord that I'm working for Him to the best of my ability. I pray that God will give me a chance to pray to Him the way I like to pray to Him. If I pray by making soup and serving soup, I feel I'm praying by doing. When I'm in bed, and the doctor has told me firmly to stay there for a few days, I don't feel I've earned my right to pray for myself and others, to pray for these poor folks who come here for a square meal.

My college years were about entering alien territory intrepidly. What was a suburban, middle-class, Indian kid doing in Marxist circles and homeless shelters? I wore the unexpectedness of it all like a badge of honor. Sometimes I wondered whether shock value was more important to me than social justice.

The Catholic Workers were the least likely circle for a kid like me. They were more radical than the Marxist intellectuals I knew, more gentle than the social service types I volunteered with, more intelligent than the professors who taught my classes, and more effective than the activists I protested with. And yet I felt so at ease with them. Reading Dorothy Day, I realized why: they knew that God had created humanity with the hope that we would achieve the Kingdom on earth. Their purpose for doing this work was in their bones and emerged with every breath. Once one realizes that, what can one do but obey with joy? As William James wrote in *The Varieties of Religious Experience,* "[Faith is] the belief that there is an unseen order, and that our supreme good lies in harmoniously adjusting ourselves thereto."

One of my discomforts with radical politics was that it deified the individual. The underlying belief of all the radicals I knew was that our reasons, our methods, our ability to help others all came from our own minds. We were so smart and smug. I even felt a peculiar similarity with the Jeopardy battles my friends and I had had in high school, except the game with my radical friends was who could most elegantly apply Fanon to current events. Day's view that God is the source of love, equality, and connection—and that He requires His ultimate creation, humanity, to achieve the same on earth—made sense to me in a deep place, perhaps the same place I was trying to fill in high school by fasting.

When Catholic Workers asked about my religion, I told them that I didn't really have one. They were happy for me to participate in their prayer life anyway, and they made it clear that I should do whatever felt comfortable to me and no more. I found the singing and praying and moments of silence deeply inspiring. I bowed my head and followed along as best I could. But I always found myself standing at a slight angle to the core symbols of the Christian faith—the Cross, the blood, the Resurrection—and I never felt any desire to convert. Nobody in the Catholic Worker movement ever suggested that I do so.

They saved me just the same. I realized this years later, when I met Bill Ayers. I was working in Chicago and interested in new models of youth development. Several people suggested I go see Bill, a Distinguished Professor of Education at the University of Illinois at Chicago and a key figure in both local school reform and the small schools movement. "Where have I heard that name before?" I thought, and suddenly I made the connection to the Weather Underground, the radical sixties group that had planted bombs in federal buildings as a strategy for bringing down the system.

Bill had recently published his memoir, *Fugitive Days*. The similarities between our stories was scary. We were both middle-class kids from Glen Ellyn who had discovered the dark side of America in college and responded with rage. We both had contempt for liberals and romanticized the violent rebellions of John Brown and Che Guevara. We were both familiar with the Jeffersonian line that the people should rebel during every era. We both fancied ourselves in the vanguard.

Sitting at the kitchen table one night in 1968, talking about the death machine that was the U.S. government, a new guy in Bill's circle, Terry Robbins, had suggested that things had gone too far and it was time to bomb the pigs into the Stone Age. At first Bill and his friends resisted. That's crazy, they said. "There's got to be a place in this revolution for a man of principled violence," Terry responded. Bill found the image intoxicating, and he spent the ensuing years doing violent battle with cops, learning to build bombs, and calling for all "mother country radicals" to bring the war home with acts of violence on American soil. He lost several friends and a decade of his life in the process.

What if I had been at that kitchen table that night? What if a Terry Robbins figure had crossed my path, showed me his sketchbook full of bomb designs, encouraged me to study the *Blaster's Handbook*? At nineteen, I was already convinced that America understood only violence. I was just this side of believing that it was my responsibility to inflict it. I only needed a nudge.

My father couldn't make it all the way through *Fugitive Days*. "It reminds me too much of you," he said. "It scares the shit out of me, what you could have become."

It had been chance—grace—that I had sat at the Catholic Worker table and it had been Dorothy Day's book that had fallen into my hands.

On our summer road trip, Sarah and I visited Emily Shihadeh in San Francisco. She received us warmly, with big hugs, and after spending a few minutes with Sarah, she declared that taking her advice and making my move was the smartest thing I had ever done. Then came the platefuls of hummus, falafel, and pita. "I love Middle Eastern food," Sarah said.

"This is Arab food, Palestinian food," Emily responded, growing suddenly cool. "The Israelis occupy our land, but they cannot take our culture."

Sarah understood that comment in context, as illustrative of the sentiment of the people who had lost something, in some cases everything, when Israel had triumphed. She did not grow defensive or angry. Instead, she resolved to explore the Palestinian side of the matter during her semester in Israel.

I visited her in Israel, at Hebrew University on Mount Scopus, where a few years later a close friend of hers was in the cafeteria during a suicide bombing. We floated in the Dead Sea, wandered through Jerusalem's markets (where Sarah bought a plaque for my parents with IN THE NAME OF GOD written in Arabic on it), ate hot bagels with savory zatar (an aromatic spice mixture), went to the Wailing Wall and the Dome of the Rock, visited the Way of the Cross. In Haifa, we walked through the gardens of the Baha'i Temple and listened to an earnest young man in pleated khaki pants tell us about the need for unity.

Sarah delved into the Palestinian situation and into Jewish history in Israel. She was heartbroken by both. I knew little about either. Sarah took me on a tour of the Arab neighborhoods in East Jerusalem. The tour guide was a friend of hers, a young American Jew who had moved to Israel, what Jews call "making aliyah." He and the Arab kids who gathered spoke in both Hebrew and Arabic, talking about life in Arab villages, the simple pleasures of backgammon games and Arabic coffee on Sunday afternoons, the frustration of waiting for hours at Israeli checkpoints on their way to visit family in the West Bank. Sarah put her hands over her face when she heard this. "I hate that their lives are like this," she told me later.

Our tour guide at Yad Vashem, the Israeli Holocaust memorial, was another American who had made aliyah. He came across as a smooth intellectual, mentioning his two PhDs in passing. After he had caught us in the web of his seductive intellect, he carefully injected his right-wing poison. He told stories of the destruction of Kristallnacht, the livelihoods lost, the intimidation of children and women in Jewish neighborhoods, the fear of men that it would only get worse. He ended the story in a flat voice, saying that the world had done nothing then, and why should Jews expect the world to pay attention to their suffering now? He walked us through the various halls of Yad Vashem, telling more stories of suffering, bringing half the group to tears, and continuing to press his particular politics. "Oslo," he said, and shook his head in disgust. "Haven't we Jews heard this before? Land for peace. It didn't work when Neville Chamberlain, that spineless wimp, tried it sixty years ago. Look what it led to then. Who can believe it will lead to something different now?"

I knew little about international peacemaking and nothing about the Oslo Accords, signed by Israel and the Palestine Liberation Organization (PLO) in September 1993, but I could tell a spoiler when I saw one. Sarah was as furious with him as I was. "There are so many people who are trying to create a just situation here, and people like him are working to defeat us every day," she told me on the way out.

Jewish identity issues had always played a large role in Sarah's life, and they became paramount in Israel. "The most important thing to people here is that you marry another Jew," she told me. "The intermarriage rate between Jews and non-Jews is so high now that some Jewish leaders are saying that the Jews are killing Judaism ourselves. They would rather a Jew eat a bacon double cheeseburger than marry outside the faith." In her own gentle way, Sarah was telling me that she was struggling with our relationship. She felt as if she had an obligation to her tradition, her people. I was too daft to catch her drift.

We went to a Shabbat dinner in Jerusalem with a group of young

American and Israeli Jews. The conversation shifted back and forth between graduate school plans and social justice issues. These were the things that college students and recent graduates talked about all the time. I felt completely at home. I wound up in a conversation with a young Jewish woman in a long skirt. It looked like a religious outfit. I asked her about it, and she explained to me that she was an Orthodox Jew and followed a tradition called *shomer negiah*. In her community, unmarried men and women could not date, could not touch, could not be in the same room together unsupervised. "I will marry a Jew," she told me with total certainty, "and I will do it according to the dictates of my tradition."

She motioned toward Sarah and said, "The girl you came with, she is your girlfriend? She is a Jew?"

"Yes," I said.

"And you, what are you?"

"Nothing really, I guess. I'm exploring different spiritualities right now," I told her.

"Will you and Sarah marry?" she asked.

"Um, we don't really talk about that right now," I said. "I mean, we're together. That feels like a lot for where we are at in our lives."

"Oh," she said, looking at me with some suspicion. I realized that she was younger than both Sarah and me, but she did not consider marriage too much of a responsibility for her. It would be an honor and a duty for her to be married; it would be carrying out the will of her community and continuing with the practices of her tradition.

"And if you get married, what will your wedding be like? Whose tradition will it follow?"

I shrugged. It wasn't something I had thought about. It didn't seem important.

Sarah had been listening to our conversation, and I could feel her getting increasingly uncomfortable. At the mention of our wedding, she got up abruptly, disrupting the conversation she was in, and said to me, "I want to go." I could tell she was mad, but I had no idea why. I got our coats, hailed a taxi, and waited for her to lay into me.

"Do you have any idea what you were doing tonight?" she said. "That girl you were talking to is a devout Orthodox Jew. She lives by rules that were handed down by God. She is part of a tradition that is thousands of years old. Every question she asked you was a ridiculing of me. There was an invisible conversation that you were totally oblivious to, whose main theme was that Sarah is a bad Jew because she is dating a goy. The only reason she kept on asking you questions was to get more details on how wayward I am."

I wanted to say, "Screw her. Why does she get to tell you what to do?" And then I realized something: Sarah *wanted* that. She had come to Israel to connect with her community, her tradition. What is a community but a group of people who have some claim over you, and what is a tradition but a set of stories and principles and rules handed down over hundreds or thousands of years that each new generation has to wrestle with?

I started sobbing. The cabdriver must have thought we were crazy. Sarah, warm and sweet, moved over to me and put her hand on my back. I had totally lost it by this point, weeping uncontrollably, as if a loved one had died.

"What is it, my love?" Sarah asked.

I finally pulled myself together. "It's just that you feel like you have something to live up to, this Judaism thing. You have these principles you talk about, and this community that watches out for you, and even when it feels suffocating, at least you know they care for you. I have none of that. I just have some things that I'm interested in and a bunch of groups I come in and out of. But I could leave them at any time, and they wouldn't know I was gone."

It was a harsh truth I was telling. For all my talk of identity politics, I had yet to develop much of an identity.

4
Real World Activism

> We may either smother the divine
> fire of youth or we may feed it.
> JANE ADDAMS

Brother Wayne Teasdale had two great hopes for me: that I would start an interfaith youth movement and that I would take mushrooms with him. He got one.

I met Brother Wayne in the spring of 1997. In addition to being a Catholic monk, Brother Wayne had a PhD in philosophy and had spent years at an ashram in India, where he took vows in a Hindu monastic tradition. He was also on the board of the Council for a Parliament of the World's Religions, an international interfaith organization based in Chicago.

Brother Wayne fascinated me. He had a head of gray hair but the spirit of an idealistic teenager, easily thrilled and totally devoid of cynicism. He seemed a cross between Don Quixote, Zorba the Greek, Saint Francis of Assisi, and the mad scientist from the *Back to the Future* movies. "Come see me in Hyde Park," he said when we met. I jumped at the chance.

He lived in a small apartment in the Catholic Theological Union complex. Books on Christian theology, pictures of Hindu deities, and CDs of Indian classical music were strewn everywhere. Brother Wayne cleared a small place near the window and announced that it was time to meditate. A ticking clock bothered him. I heard him get up to put it away. When we were done meditating, I saw him retrieve it from the freezer.

"Time for a walk," he said. We pulled on our sweaters and headed south down Cornell Avenue. We passed a dog. Brother Wayne bent down and rubbed the dog's head. The dog wagged its tail and barked. "That is a very spiritual dog," Brother Wayne told me as we ambled on. "I know most of the dogs in this neighborhood," he added.

We continued our walk until we came to a man wearing a heavy winter coat and carrying a black garbage bag with aluminum cans. "Hey, Wayne," he said. "Ralph, it's so nice to see you," Brother Wayne replied. They caught up. Brother Wayne took out his wallet and handed Ralph a twenty. "Ralph is a very spiritual man," he said. "I know most of the homeless people in this neighborhood."

We entered a café, ordered, and sat down. A man from outside saw Brother Wayne, waved frantically, and bounded in. "I've told you before," scolded the girl at the counter, "no public restroom."

He looked at Brother Wayne. Brother Wayne nodded. "Coffee," the man said triumphantly. "Large," he said with glee. The man sat down at our table. The girl brought the coffee. Brother Wayne handed over $2. The man launched into a screeching rant about how Mayor Richard Daley was putting poison in the water supply. Brother Wayne listened. "Now, Harold, perhaps you should—" Harold cut him off and started in on the Clinton administration.

I grabbed a newspaper from the next table. Brother Wayne listened some more. We finished our coffee. Brother Wayne and Harold hugged. I offered a polite, somewhat standoffish hand. Harold pumped it. Brother Wayne and I headed back to his apartment. "Harold has a spiritual side, but sometimes it's hard to see," Brother Wayne explained. I half expected him to add that he knew most of the raving lunatics in the neighborhood.

Somehow, in between these various encounters, I got the story of why Brother Wayne was interested in me. He was convinced that we were experiencing the interspiritual moment in human history, a time when the great religions of the world would come together to affirm their common values. He wanted more action from the interfaith movement, particularly around environmental issues and freeing Tibet. But after more than a decade of involvement with interfaith organizations, Brother Wayne had lost hope that the existing leaders of the interfaith movement would take bold steps. "They are all very spiritual people," he explained to me, "but they are afraid of exercising their prophetic voice." So he had set out to find new blood.

Then he turned to me and said with utter seriousness, "I think you can play a leadership role in the global interfaith youth movement. I can tell you are a very spiritual person."

"Sure," I told him. Who can say no to that?

I had been in Chicago for about six months. I had spent the summer after graduating from college traveling around the United States with Sarah. We drove from New York City across to Seattle, down to San Francisco, and then back to Chicago, hiking in national parks, hanging out in the bohemian areas of cities, and volunteering at Catholic Worker houses along the way. Unlike my friends, who despite their radical politics had all locked up jobs before graduating or been accepted to graduate school, I came back to Chicago in mid-August 1996 with a firm commitment to do something good but no concrete plans. I discovered the St. Francis Catholic Worker House on the North Side of the city. All the rooms were taken, but I was welcome to the couch in the front area. Be warned, Ruthie told me, the cats have a proprietary interest in it; the window is drafty; and Jimmy, one of the residents, gets phone calls from his imaginary friends in the middle of the night and argues loudly with them until dawn. It sounded like home to me. I moved in and started looking for a job.

I found exactly what I was looking for: a teaching position at an alternative education program for urban minority high school dropouts on the near northwest side of Chicago. A friend of mine who knew a departing teacher at the school told me they were hiring. I showed up on graduation day, stayed through the ceremony, and sat in a chair outside the school director's office until she returned. She looked at my résumé, noticed that I had no teaching experience, and pointed out that, at twenty, I would be younger than many of my students. "I will do everything in my power to be an effective teacher here," I told her. Only one teacher was staying at the school. The school director was desperate, and I guess I was convincing enough to take a chance on.

The school was a program of the Association House of Chicago, a large social service agency inspired by Jane Addams's Hull House. We were located on North Avenue in between Damen and Western, right on the border between the two gang nations that define growing up in Chicago for too many urban teenagers. The neighborhood, Wicker Park, was fast gentrifying. Streetlights, coffee shops, and vegetarian restaurants were moving in, and working-class people of color were heading west in search of affordable rents.

Called El Cuarto Año, or "the fourth year," the school was expected to take high school dropouts who read at a fifth-grade level and prepare them to pass the general equivalency diploma, or GED, exam within six months. That would have been an impossible task if our students had an ideal support system. Most didn't. Many of our male students were involved in gangs, and some had already done stints in the juvenile detention facility. Most of our female students had at least one baby. The vast majority were poor, many were in the process of being uprooted by Wicker Park's gentrification, and none of them had had good experiences in school. Safety, baby-sitting, basic nutrition, and self-confidence were all issues that had to be addressed along with education.

I was absolutely confident. Had I not read radical education theory? Did I not have deep insights into urban poverty and youth development based on my advanced sociology classes? Was I not the founder of several tutoring programs for elementary school children in my college town? I barely paid attention to any of the discussion in the faculty meetings. I planned to run my classroom my way. When the students started complaining that other teachers were boring and ineffective compared to me, my colleagues would be prepared for me to show them how to be a *real* ghetto teacher. I figured it would happen by October.

As part of its retention strategy, El Cuarto Año required each student to identify a support person—a parent, an older sibling, a romantic partner. In the meetings I held with prospective students and their support people prior to the beginning of the school year, I spent a good chunk of time explaining that I understood why they had been unsuccessful in school. I emphasized that the system had been designed to fail them. I cited Jonathan Kozol and William Ryan on the chronic underfunding of urban schools due to unfair tax policy. I talked about bell hooks's theory that the legacy of racism and the odor of colonialism deeply impact the attitude of students of color toward school, which they associate with white supremacy. I assured them that I would be taking a Freireian approach to teaching, using the knowledge base that my students brought into the classroom. And just to put their minds at ease, I confirmed that Ebonics was not only allowed but encouraged in my classroom.

After hearing my lecture, one parent asked, "You're going to teach my daughter how to read, right?"

I realized that I had skipped that part. In fact, I had hardly thought about it at all. My liberal arts education had provided me with ways to understand what was wrong with the world but few skills to help put it right. My own arrogance had prevented me from seeking effective practical methods of helping urban minority high school dropouts get an education. In a week, I would face a classroom full of challenging students, and I had no idea how to teach them. My confidence quickly gave way to fear.

I became a teacher the hard way: by designing ineffective lesson plans, having my students sneer when I taught them, and working until midnight to adjust the next day's plan so that I didn't make the same mistakes as I had the day before. I learned how important it is to start class on time, to demand that all assignments be completed in neat penmanship, and to assign books that both challenged and appealed to my students.

Sometimes I took a break during my midnight lesson-planning sessions and imagined one of my college professors teaching my class. I couldn't help but laugh at the vision of some of the nation's leading experts on minority education and urban sociology faced with teaching the students about whom they theorized. Nearly every course I took in college had begun with the professor saying that his or her main goal was to make us "critical thinkers." I brought that same view to my classroom and spent a lot of time explaining structural racism and the legacy of colonialism.

But my students at El Cuarto Año were experts on inequality. They didn't need to hear from me that the hand they got dealt was unfair. What they needed was somebody who could teach them basic, useful skills: algebra, reading comprehension, essay composition. Then they would have what my suburban education gave me: the tools to make up my own mind about the world around me. I began wishing that my professors had spent a little more time lecturing on how to constructively engage the world as it is and a little less time teaching me how to criticize it.

More than anything else, I was amazed by how extensively gang violence pervaded my students' lives. Some of them couldn't ride the bus or train to school for fear of encountering rival gang members. Others wouldn't come to school for days at a time because of a gang obligation. "I had an operation," they would say when they showed up a week later. That was code for being called on by a gang leader to join an organized battle with another gang, sometimes across the street, sometimes across the city.

I remember tutoring Jose after school one day and noticing a perfectly round hole in his jeans. "What's that?" I asked.

"That's where I got shot, dog," he said, pride filling his voice. "It was a battle at Leavitt and LeMoyne, when the Kings used to own that corner." He showed me the pitchfork he had tattooed on his arm, the sign of the Latin Kings.

"I don't get it," I told him. "Are you telling me the same guy who is sitting here reading poetry by William Blake stands on street corners with a gun because of that little sign?"

"You think the school I went to had teachers that stayed after for tutoring sessions? Man, the teachers at that school didn't even show up half the time. We'd have some stupid sub up there in the front of the room yelling at us to do a worksheet, same damn worksheet yesterday's sub gave us to do. Since I was six years old, everybody around me be asking 'What gang you ride? What gang you ride?' Nobody asked, 'What poetry you read? What level of math you at?' One day, you decide you might as well ride *something*, or else you nobody to no one. So you choose one. Then you hated by half and loved by half. But at least you *somebody*."

In early November, I left the St. Francis Catholic Worker House. I had a constant cold as a result of the drafty window, a bunch of scratches on my arm from the cat, and continual sleep deprivation thanks to Jimmy's late-night conversations with his imaginary friends, which had gotten louder and louder as Jimmy had gotten deafer and deafer. I had met another recent college graduate through activist circles in Chicago, and the two of us found an apartment together.

I was making progress as a teacher. School no longer felt like a battle. My students' reading and writing skills were improving dramatically. Many did earn their GEDs, several continued their education at local community colleges, and a couple even went directly on to De-Paul University. But it was a lonely existence. I felt as if I was bursting with stories from school and had nobody to tell them to. My $12,000 salary prevented me from being a regular part of the dinner-and-a-show social scene that some of my friends with higher-paying jobs were in. What I really missed was a community, a setup where sharing a story or asking a question was just a walk down the hall away.

On New Year's Day 1997, I resolved to address the problem directly. I suggested to my roommate that we host a potluck for our generation of activists in Chicago—teachers, social workers, environmentalists, community organizers, whatever. Six people showed up on the first Tuesday in February. I cooked masala potatoes, the only dish I knew how to make (a fact that is, sadly, still true). We talked about typical activist stuff—the gentrification happening in the city, the centrist mode of the Democratic Party—but mostly we exchanged stories and had laughs. We had all gone through the experience of taking a set of ideals we had gathered as undergraduates and trying to apply them in this postcollege life.

"When are we going to do this again?" asked my friend Jeff from Allen Hall, who was working as a community organizer in a Latino neighborhood of Chicago.

"Next week," I offered.

And so it became a ritual. Every Tuesday I would wake up excited, get home early, cook my potatoes, and wait for my activist friends to start showing up around 7:00 p.m. The numbers grew, from the original six, to their immediate circle of friends, to those people's circles, and on and on. People on the South Side of Chicago heard about the Tuesday night potlucks and started coming up to the North Side for the vegetarian food and conversation. People had friends at universities in the Midwest, at Michigan and Illinois and Wisconsin, and they dropped by during their spring breaks. By the time the weather got warm, we were spilling out into the front yard. At one point, there must have been eighty people there. They brought poems to share, instruments to play, and news from activists organizing students and workers in out-of-the-way places.

While washing dishes around ten one night, I overheard a conversation behind me. "I live for Tuesday nights," one person said.

"Me, too," another said. "This is the only place where I feel people get what I'm about. I wish we could have this energy on a 24-7 basis."

"You mean live together?" a third asked. "This ain't the sixties, man. That doesn't happen anymore."

I turned around. "Sure it does. Ever heard of the Catholic Worker movement? Their whole thing is based on the idea of people with social justice values living together in community and serving others."

Our conversation was beginning to attract attention. A couple of people who had graduated from the University of Wisconsin piped in. "It happens in Madison, too. There's a whole system of cooperatives up there where students and local activists live together, buy food in bulk, share chores, and generally energize each other to do good in the world." The idea started taking shape.

We decided to ask a senior Chicago activist, Kathy Kelly, founder of an organization called Voices in the Wilderness that opposed sanctions and war on Iraq, to come by the following week and give us some advice on making this idea a reality. Kathy was overjoyed to hear a group of young activists in Chicago talk about forming a social justice community. She told us about a Catholic parish in the Uptown neighborhood with an almost empty convent. Most of the nuns had left, and the priest was considering renting it. We better hurry, Kathy warned us; other people were interested in the building as well.

About six of us were committed to the idea of forming a community. We started meeting every Sunday night to figure out the shape of the project. We put together a mission statement, decided that community decisions would be made by consensus, and crafted a process for admitting new members.

"I love this," Linda said during one meeting. "We each bring something important and unique to this discussion. Mark and Allie have the experience of living in co-ops in Madison. Eboo and Jeff know about the Catholic Worker movement. It reminds me of my favorite childhood story, about a guy who comes into a starving village with a large pot and a big stone and tells the villagers that he is going to cook them stone soup. He puts water and the stone in a pot, and when it starts boiling, he tastes it and says, 'It's almost ready, but it needs some carrots.' One of the villagers says that he has some carrots, and he runs and gets those. The guy cuts them up, puts them in the pot, and then tastes it again and says, 'Almost ready. It just needs some celery.' Somebody else says they've got celery and runs and gets it, and the guy cuts it up and puts it in the pot. And on and on with potatoes and turnips and garlic. And then presto—stone soup."

People were quiet for a moment. The story had struck a profound chord. "I think that's exactly what we're about," Jeff said. "Creating a space that brings out the various talents of a diverse community, and then collecting those talents so that they form something even better that can feed all of us."

"I think we just got our name—Stone Soup," John said.

A small group of us went to meet with Father Lambert from Our Lady of Lourdes Parish. We described the mission of Stone Soup and told him that each of us was actively helping others through our professional work. What we were about resonated with him, but he preferred to rent his convent to a religious group. "Are any of you Catholic?" he asked.

Nobody raised a hand.

"Anybody Christian?"

A couple of people said they had been raised Christian.

"Anybody religious?"

Nobody.

He paused for a long time. "Well, your mission certainly has a spiritual core. I am going to get scrutinized for this move by the archdiocese, but I think I'm willing to give it a try."

Seven of us moved into the Stone Soup Cooperative on Ashland in the Uptown neighborhood of Chicago in September 1997. Our membership grew to fifteen that first year. Our Tuesday night potlucks regularly drew fifty-plus people, including some of the most cutting-edge young activists and artists in the city. We were covered by the *Chicago Tribune*, Chicago Public Radio, and the *Chicago Reader* (the city's alternative weekly, which referred to Stone Soup as a community "that smelled strongly of lentils"). Stone Soup started playing a role in neighborhood affairs, especially in doing our best to keep Uptown economically and ethnically diverse. A small group of forward-thinking people started pooling their money, and when, un-expectedly, a large house down the street went on the market, they had several thousand dollars toward a down payment on a site that would become Stone Soup II, the Leland House.

Somebody once asked me for a metaphor to describe Stone Soup, and I said it was the love child of Walt Whitman and Ani DiFranco. It was the most creative group of people I have ever been around, the most fun I have ever had. But there was a part of me that it did not fill. At Stone Soup, we rejoiced in creating ourselves anew every day. The lightness of that was not so much unbearable as unsatisfying. Occa-sionally, I would think about Sarah in Israel, and I wondered what it might be like to feel the weight of history. I loved my work as a teacher, and I loved the people I was living with, but however I combined com-munity, justice, and creativity, it did not add up to identity.

And that was one of the key reasons I was attracted to Brother Wayne. He might have had his head in the clouds, but he had a very clear sense of his role in the cosmos.

My friend Kevin and I started tagging along with Brother Wayne to various interfaith events. Everywhere he went, Brother Wayne was adored, treated like a holy man rock star. After finishing his talk, Brother Wayne would invite Kevin and me to the stage. "These are the leaders of the next generation, a Muslim and a Jew who are build-ing the interfaith youth movement," he would say. Then he would move away from the microphone and whisper to us, "Tell them about the interfaith youth movement."

There were three problems with the position Brother Wayne put us in. First, Kevin and I were uncomfortable with being called a Mus-lim and a Jew. Actually, we were both trying to be Buddhists. One of the reasons we were drawn to Brother Wayne was his intimate knowl-edge of Eastern traditions. He was very close friends with the Dalai Lama's brother and had recently entered into a dialogue with His Holiness himself. Kevin and I wanted him to teach us meditation, chanting, secrets, anything that seemed mysterious. The last thing we wanted was to be boxed into the traditions of our birth. We still harbored an adolescent discrimination against the familiar.

But Brother Wayne didn't see boxes or borders. He happily taught us meditation techniques and introduced us to Hindu and Buddhist writers. He had spent years studying both traditions, and the encounter with them had served to strengthen his Catholic faith and help him rethink it along the way. He was, after all, a monk who taught at a Catholic seminary, took his vows very seriously, and had received a special honor from Chicago's archbishop, Francis Cardinal George. The tradition you were born into was your home, Brother Wayne told me, but as Gandhi once wrote, it should be a home with the windows open so that the winds of other traditions can blow through and bring their unique oxygen. "It's good to have wings," he would say, "but you have to have roots, too."

The second problem with the position Brother Wayne put Kevin and me in was that there was no interfaith youth movement, at least none that Kevin and I knew about. We were two twentysomethings in Chicago exploring spirituality, diversity, community, and social justice. That hardly constituted a movement. Still, when Brother Wayne invited us to speak, we would look at each other and shrug and move to the mike. What else could we do but talk? "It's like free-styling," Kevin would say later, using a hip-hop term for making the story up as you go along, as long as it contains the truth.

We ended up articulating a zigzag of hopes. Shouldn't we look at poetry and scripture from different religions and try to find the common pulse of love that ran through them? Shouldn't we bring young people from radically different backgrounds—rich and poor, Easterner and Westerner, Arab and American—together to build community in diversity? Shouldn't we follow the lead of Martin Luther King Jr. and Abraham Joshua Heschel, a Christian and a Jew, who had marched together in Selma, Alabama, for freedom, Heschel even saying, "I felt like my legs were praying"?

People loved our free-styling. We regularly got standing ovations.

Teachers would ask us to speak to their classes. Religious leaders wanted us to visit their congregations.

We started to feel a little uncomfortable with the attention. At one point, I made a confession to Brother Wayne: "There really isn't an interfaith youth movement. Kevin and I are just dreaming out loud."

He was unperturbed. "Even articulating the hope is helping to make it a reality. Keep praying for it and meeting people who feel like you do, and it will begin to take shape."

The third problem with going to these events was that they were excruciatingly boring. They were always dinners or conferences with a lot of old people doing a lot of talking. The big goal seemed to be drafting documents declaring that religious people should be dialoguing with each other and then planning the next conference for the document to be reviewed. It was always the same people saying the same things, and still the events went way too long. I remember one especially torturous interfaith dinner in Chicago. By the time the ninth speaker of the evening took the podium, the audience was long past being discreet about looking at their watches and had begun to shift noisily in their seats. The evening had proceeded like most interfaith activities: a couple of hundred people ranging from middle-aged to senior citizen picking at plates of dry hotel food and listening to a long list of speakers repeat the same reasons interfaith activities are important. This speaker, a senior American religious leader, appeared to notice the restlessness and tried to bring new energy to the crowd. In a kind of singsongy shout, he declared, "This is so important what we are doing here. It is interfaith we are doing." He paused while a look of delight crossed his face. "Yes, interfaith is a doing. It is a verb. Repeat after me," he said gleefully. "We are interfaithing."

"Interfaithing," mumbled about half the audience. The rest stared longingly at the door. Pretending not to notice the halfhearted response, the speaker plowed ahead through the reasons we must continue having annual interfaith banquets. "See you next year," he said with a satisfied air.

Not only was I bored at these events, but I was also deflated. I wanted so badly to be part of a movement that brought spirituality, diversity, and social action together in a very concrete way. At the heart of every social movement I studied—the civil rights movement, the struggle against apartheid in South Africa, the movement to free India—had been a group of religiously diverse people putting their skins on the line for social justice. Every leader I admired was deeply rooted in a different faith. I could not understand why the people at the interfaith events I attended seemed so thrilled that Buddhists, Hindus, Jews, Christians, and Muslims had all gathered at one conference. My high school lunch table had had at least as much diversity. It baffled me that so much energy was spent on writing documents and creating interfaith ceremonies and positioning people onstage ever so carefully so that the photographs could come out looking like a Benetton ad. Where was the concrete commitment to social action, the stuff that our faith heroes had been about? And where were the young people?

Kevin and I were about fed up with interfaith events when we got a phone call from Charles Gibbs, the executive director of the United Religions Initiative (URI), an international interfaith organization based in San Francisco. Brother Wayne had told Charles that the interfaith movement had to involve more young people and that Kevin and I were building an interfaith youth movement in Chicago. Charles was calling to invite us to the URI's Global Summit. He gave us full scholarships to the conference and told us that there were going to be young people there from around the world who were interested in being part of the interfaith youth movement.

The URI had been formed in the mid-1990s by William Swing, then the Episcopal bishop of the diocese of California. The big idea was that interfaith work needed to include not just high-level religious leaders but also people at the grass roots, and that there had to be concrete, ongoing interfaith activities and not just international conferences. The job of a global organization would be to network various local interfaith groups and coordinate their activities.

The URI Global Summit was held at Stanford and was attended

by people from several dozen countries around the world. The under-thirties skipped a lot of the conference sessions to spend time together. We had come from Malaysia, Ghana, Brazil, Argentina, and the United States. We were Hindus, Jews, Christians, Muslims, Baha'is, Buddhists, and practitioners of indigenous religions. In the discussions of our faith lives, two themes stood out: our faith formation had occurred in the midst of religious diversity, and serving others was a core part of how we lived our religions. A young Hindu woman called herself a "karma yogi," someone who seeks God through the path of actively serving others. Kevin talked about the connection between the Hindu call to service and the Jewish command of *tikkun olam*, repairing the world. A Malaysian Christian quoted from Matthew 25 and said that this is exactly what Jesus was about. I couldn't help but think of the conversation I had had with my parents about volunteering and their insistence that I serve because it was part of Islam.

The discussions went long into the night, and by the time I got back to my room, I was exhausted. But I couldn't sleep. It was a rare space that we had created at that conference: an open conversation about faith, diversity, and service. In other spaces, I had experienced pieces of these conversations, but never all the parts together. In college, I had been part of a lot of service learning efforts that brought people from diverse backgrounds together to build houses or tutor children, but we had never talked about faith. At Catholic Worker houses, there was much discussion of faith and service, but little talk of religious diversity. Thus far, my experience in the interfaith movement had included plenty of faith and diversity, but little attention to concrete service.

I was afraid that space would evaporate with the goodbye hugs at the end of the conference. How to continue it? I racked my brain late at night thinking about that. And suddenly, an idea hit me: what if we created a project where religiously diverse young people came together for one year in a residential community where they would live together and take part in community service projects? There were a number of faith-based efforts along these lines—Jesuit Volunteer

Corps, Lutheran Volunteer Corps, and a parallel Jewish volunteer program called Avodah. They connected faith and service but had no religious diversity. Moreover, there were programs like City Year, Teach for America, and Public Allies that deliberately brought people from different races, classes, genders, and geographic backgrounds together to engage in community development efforts (although they were generally not residential programs), but faith was largely ignored. And then there was the interfaith movement, where people from different religious backgrounds came together, but they seemed intent on focusing on organizing conferences, curating ceremonies, and drafting documents. An Interfaith Youth Corps would learn from all of these efforts while creating something genuinely new.

It was about three in the morning. Four more hours, and I would be able to tell other people about this.

Ideas become reality when the right people commit to them. There are two categories of the "right people"—mentors and peers. Mentors are people with resources, networks, and wisdom. They guide you, encourage you, and connect you. In *One Day, All Children . . .* , Wendy Kopp describes the various mentors who helped launch Teach for America. The chair of Princeton's sociology department, Marvin Bressler, immediately saw the potential of the idea. He set up a meeting with Princeton's director of development so that Wendy could learn about fundraising. The director of development agreed to have Princeton act as Teach for America's fiscal agent. Richard Fisher, a fellow Princeton alum and the CEO of Morgan Stanley, gave Wendy a sympathetic ear and free office space. The founders of City Year, Michael Brown and Alan Khazei, provided ongoing strategic advice, including the all-important counsel "Just say no" when other people ask you to change your mission even a tiny bit. The little things made a big difference. Wendy writes about a corporate executive who called her and said, "Wendy, I just read your proposal. It's stunning." That phone call energized her for a week.

Thankfully, the URI Global Summit was a world of friendly mentors. Charles Gibbs had watched the young people sneak out of conference sessions with a twinkle in his eye. When I cornered him at breakfast with the idea of the Interfaith Youth Corps, he said, "I was wondering what you all were cooking up." Jim Kenney, a longtime supporter of youth participation in interfaith work, listened intently to the idea and suggested a practical next step: that different interfaith organizations contribute money to a youth conference where the details could be further discussed. Joe Hall, a conference participant who came from a community development and arts background, spent an entire afternoon with me discussing how to make this idea happen. He gave me exactly what I needed at the time: his belief that the Interfaith Youth Corps idea was both powerful and possible, and his counsel that anger-based activism goes only a fraction of the distance that compassion-based approaches do.

Even more important than the support of mentors, I needed the companionship of my peers. I wanted to make sure that I wasn't crazy when I said that young people desired a space to connect faith, diversity, and service and that my initial sketch for an Interfaith Youth Corps met that need. Wendy Kopp writes that throughout all the early trials of creating Teach for America, her most important connection was to her peers who were committed to educational equality in America. I felt the same love from my peers at the Global Summit. "That's exactly what our generation needs to be about," said my friend Parthi, a Malaysian Christian. "Yeah, man, make that thing happen," said Socrates, an African Traditionalist from Ghana. Our conference discussions began focusing on the shape of this project. As the end of the conference loomed, a big question hung in the air: who would do what when we all scattered back home? I repeated the offer made by Jim Kenney and Charles Gibbs to help fund an interfaith youth conference and committed to take the lead on it. Other people stated what they could do. I left the conference with an idea, a burning passion, and a group of mentors and peers ready to making it a reality.

Kevin and I went to see Brother Wayne about the Interfaith Youth Corps as soon as we got back to Chicago. He could barely contain himself as we described it. When he finally calmed down, he started plotting strategy. "Well, after the corps frees Tibet, it can start working on the environment. Those are the two biggest crises of our time, and their causes are spiritual. The solutions have to be spiritual, too."

He was quiet for a moment. "You know who will want to hear about this?" he suddenly said. "His Holiness." He stood up abruptly, pointed his finger in the air, and proclaimed, "You have to go to Dharamsala and tell His Holiness about the Interfaith Youth Corps. You have to get his blessing before you do anything else."

5
An American in India

What is my inheritance? To what am I an heir?
To all that humanity has achieved during tens of
thousands of years, to all that it has thought and
felt and suffered and taken pleasure in, to its cries
of triumph and its bitter agony of defeat, to that
astonishing adventure of man which began so long
ago and yet continues and beckons us. To all this
and more in common with all men. But there is
a special heritage for those of us of India, one
more especially applicable.

JAWAHARLAL NEHRU, *The Discovery of India*

Before boarding the plane on my previous trip to India, when I was fifteen, I asked my father if they had Frosted Flakes there. "I don't think
so," he replied. Then how could I be expected to stay for six weeks?

I was openly contemptuous of India during that family trip.
Thumbs Up Cola didn't taste at all like Coke, and the paper straw I
sucked it through was too small to get a good gulp in. There was no
shower in my grandmother's home. Bathing was a primitive affair that

consisted of putting water in a bucket and pouring it over yourself with a pitcher. The air conditioners made too much noise. The fans just blew the heat around. India was a land of filth, nuisance, and backwardness.

In Bombay, where my extended family is based, I spent my days inside my aunt's apartment reading Ayn Rand novels and outlining my college application essays. My cousins offered to take me out at night but soon got tired of my attitude. "Remember, tell them not to put ice in your drink," Bathool told me at a juice bar on Chowpatty Beach, doing her best to protect my American stomach from a case of the runs. "What the hell is wrong with this place that you can't even have the ice?" I responded.

When we went touring in the north, through Agra and Jaipur, the only hour I didn't complain was when we were at the Taj Mahal. My white friends at school had asked me to tell them what it was like; I paid attention so I could report back. The rest of the time, I cursed the searing heat; the sticky dirt; the stinking, heaving crush of brown bodies around me. I threw a tantrum when I discovered that we had been bumped from our original flight and would have to wait an extra two days before returning. "I just want to go home," I whined like a five-year-old to my parents.

And now I was going back to India. Six years separated the journeys. I was embarrassed by my behavior on my previous trip, but most of all I was angry at America. After all, it was America that had seduced me into adopting its styles and its scorn, forced me to sacrifice my true heritage in a devil's bargain for acceptance, and then laughed viciously when it slowly dawned on me that I would never be anything but a second-class citizen there. But I had become wise to the ways of the empire. Who says the master's tools could not dismantle the master's house? In the very universities and bookstores of the superpower, I had discovered its malicious trickster methods. My return was a reclaiming of my lost heritage, a reuniting with my people and my land, an inhabiting of the identity that had remained in my bones even when I had tried to scrub my dark skin white. I read about Gandhi's rejection of the European mindset in favor of all things Indian and fantasized about wearing homespun and walking barefoot through rural India. I thought about Malcolm X meeting with his dark-skinned brothers in Africa and beginning his movement toward Pan-Africanism, and I wondered whether, after this sojourn to my motherland, I might not do the same.

The servants were awake when Kevin and I arrived in the middle of the night at my grandmother's place in Colaba, a bustling neighborhood in South Bombay. They were huddled around the television, watching reruns of *Diff'rent Strokes* dubbed in Hindi. They cried when they saw me, the two older ones taking turns kissing and hugging and reaching up to touch my face. "They took care of you when you were a baby, and now they are seeing you grown," my grandmother explained. "That is why they are crying. They have been with our family for nearly fifty years. This one, Nassir bhai, he would take you on walks at night when you wouldn't sleep. And that one, Amin bai, she would sit and feed you your food and be so patient when you refused to eat. They did the same for your father when he was a little boy." My grandmother then put a garland of flowers around my neck and welcomed me home: "This is your city; this is your apartment. Sit, be comfortable." My cousins came; my aunts arrived. More hugs, more tears, more cheek pinching and head patting. I was home.

After breakfast, Kevin and I were ready for India. "We want to go buy Indian clothes," I told my family.

"But the best blue jeans you get in the States," my cousin Saleem said. I didn't quite understand what he was saying.

"Blue jeans," he repeated, as if I hadn't heard. "That's what everybody wears here."

"I want *Indian* clothes," I repeated. "The kind my father used to wear only at night because he was too embarrassed to wear them out in America because it is a racist country."

"You mean pajamas?" Saleem asked. I gave up on him and made the same request to my grandmother.

She also looked confused but gave instructions to Amin bai to take us shopping. Kevin and I climbed into the back of a hired car with her, and off we went. It was my first encounter with the Other World.

"Watch out! Watch out!" I said, alarm rising in my voice as the driver barely missed a bicyclist on the right. Then I realized that he had swerved to avoid the bus careening down the street on our left. There were three similar near misses before we reached the first traffic light, at which point there were about three more because none of the cars, trucks, bicyclists, pedestrians, or various animals followed the signal. Each time we nearly grazed another vehicle, I let out a little yelp. The driver calmly chewed his betel nuts and spat them out the window. "American?" he asked Amin bai.

"Mmm," she grunted, and wagged her head side to side—Hindi for yes.

I decided my best strategy was to try to ignore the road and concentrate on Amin bai. She had taken care of me when I was a baby; the least I could do was find out what was happening in her life. "How are you?" I asked.

It took a moment for her to register my question, both because it tested the limits of her English and because Indian servants are generally not asked about their lives. Amin bai seemed delighted to catch me up and launched into a stream of colorful Hindi. I didn't understand a word, but I didn't want that to stop me from making a connection with my past, my people. I nodded vigorously whenever I thought it was appropriate. Amin bai must have taken it as a good sign because she kept on talking. At one point, she pointed to her mouth and smiled widely. I smiled back and nodded, overjoyed at the thought that our connection had overcome the language barrier. Amin bai paused, and her face changed from pure happiness to slight confusion. I didn't want to lose the energy, so I smiled even wider and nodded even faster. Amin bai shrugged, popped her fingers in her mouth, removed her teeth, and placed them in my hand. "Brand-new," she said, the only English she had spoken all morning, and smiled gummily.

It was Indian travel that convinced me that going native would be harder than I had thought. The eight-hour bus ride from Chandigarh to Kangra started off fine. We were amused to be sharing the vehicle with chickens in cages and a couple of small goats. The bus conductor kept on rolling and smoking funny-smelling cigarettes, and occasionally walking up the aisle to hand one to the driver. Kevin found a sadhu, a Hindu holy man who gives up all his possessions to wander and worship, in the back of the bus and did his best to have a conversation with him. The sadhu seemed delighted with his new pupil and began lecturing in a stream of mostly Hindi inflected with small amounts of English. I decided to play a little game with myself: how many minutes before one of them says a complete sentence the other understands?

We drank water. Lots of it. Gallons and gallons. It was the one piece of advice everybody gave us wherever we went. Unfortunately, they had failed to remind us of an equally important consideration: finding a bathroom. An hour into the journey, I felt myself needing to go. I surveyed the situation. The bus hadn't actually come to a complete stop yet. People seemed to get on and off while it was still moving. Was there any way to communicate my issue to the driver or conductor? I had no idea what the words were. What about sign language? Hmmm, a dangerous idea. What was I going to do, wave at the conductor and point to my groin? Maybe that was the worst type of insult you could give somebody in India. Maybe the conductor would have to kill me to preserve his honor. I decided against it.

And now the slight pressure in my bladder felt like a river roaring behind a dam. We were an hour and a half into an eight-hour journey. What had started off as a fun roller coaster ride was starting to take on dark overtones. Our bus driver insisted on passing every vehicle on our side of the road, which usually put him on a collision course with a Tata truck coming from the other direction. The two drivers would furiously honk their horns and then swerve away at the last second. The bus driver would calmly take another puff of his hashish, then prepare to do it again. This was beginning to wear on me. My ass was starting to hurt, because the seat was basically a strip of imitation leather over cheap metal. I tried to find a position that minimized the pressure on my bladder, but it hurt my back too much to stay in it. I decided I needed to involve Kevin. I interrupted his pantomime conversation with the sadhu and said, "Listen, the next time the pothead driver slows this bus down, I'm going to jump off and find a place to pee. Can you make sure the bus doesn't leave without me?"

Kevin was skeptical, but I was clear with him that Plan B would displease all creatures on the bus except possibly the goats. We are living in a world of bad choices, I told him, and I needed his help to make the best of those bad choices work. Fifteen minutes later, I saw a few people pick up their bags, grab their children, and crouch by the door, waiting to jump off when the bus hit its slowest point. I crouched with them, absolutely gleeful at the thought of the relief ahead. We jumped together. I pulled my zipper down as I ran to a concrete wall where I saw several other men peeing. There were small pools of urine everywhere, with pieces of feces lying around. It could have been heaven. I started my stream, turned to my right, and saw my bus doing its best to avoid a herd of cows as it merged back into traffic. Kevin was frantically running up and down the aisle, trying to get both the driver's attention and the conductor's, pointing to me and then to my bags, doing his best to indicate that I was still hoping to be a passenger. I saw a row of faces sitting on the bus looking at me, with slightly amused expressions.

It took an almost spiritual willpower to stop myself in midstream, chase the bus down, and zip up at the same time. Thank God for that herd of cows, or I would never have caught up to the bus. When I climbed back on, the conductor didn't even look up to acknowledge me. He just kept calmly rolling another joint.

Kevin was furious. "Don't *ever* do that again," he said. "They think I'm crazy here. This guy is never going to talk to me now." He pointed to the sadhu. It was true; the sadhu appeared to be meditating.

I was forlorn. My back was killing me, my ass felt raw, and my bladder was still about to explode. I sat down again, trying to ignore the mocking smiles of my fellow passengers. "Why don't you just focus on your fucking goats," I wanted to tell them.

A very sad thought crossed my mind. I had done all kinds of reading on the nature of exile before coming to India. I had fancied myself in the class of people who were condemned to live in a land that was not their own, like Edward Said, the Palestinian in New York City. I had spent hours musing about the concept of "home." I was especially drawn to Robert Frost's celebrated line: "Home is the place where, when you have to go there, / They have to take you in." Now I had something to contribute to that literature: if you cannot tell a bus driver that he has to stop the bus so you can take a leak, the land you are in is not your home.

I had deeper discomforts with India. To begin with, the very idea of servants. Three of them waited on my grandmother. They slept on thin mats in the living room and kitchen; ran to her when she rang the bell in her bedroom; swept the floors; cleaned the bathrooms; did the laundry and the dishes; cooked and served and took away the food. "Mama [our grandmother] lives very simply," Saleem told me when he came over for lunch one day.

"What are you talking about?" I asked. "She has three servants. Who the hell needs three servants?"

"You have no idea how the rich in this country live. They have three servants for every room, every function of the household. They have servants just to show off their status. And they treat their servants like nonhumans. These three aren't just servants," he said, gesturing toward Amin bai, Nassir bhai, and Gulshan. "They are almost a part of the family. Mama has saved their lives."

I just shook my head. All I saw was three people waiting on one person, and I couldn't get used to it. Every morning after prayers, the servants would set the table and bring us mugs of hot masala tea and plates full of fried eggs and chewy toast. After breakfast, Kevin and I would stack our plates and mugs and try to bring them to the kitchen. "No, no, no," said Gulshan, the youngest and most educated of the servants, who could read and speak English. "Cleaning is for us to do. You relax, be comfortable."

The servants never used the same bathrooms we did. They did not drink tea from the same mugs. After we finished our meals, I walked by the kitchen and saw the three of them sitting on the floor eating theirs. I couldn't help but think of Langston Hughes's poem "I, Too, Sing America," in which he imagines a day when the house slave is no longer banished to the kitchen to eat, but sits at the table with everyone else. It made me sick to watch such blatant inequality.

When Kevin and I went to the home that Mama owned in Nargol, a small village in Gujarat, two additional people suddenly materialized to take us. "They will cook and clean for you in Nargol," she told me.

When we got to the train station, they handed Kevin and me our first-class tickets and gestured that they would meet us at the end of the journey. Then the two old women picked up our bags and waddled off to the third-class compartment. I felt like a slave driver watching them go, but I was helpless to stop them.

When we arrived in Nargol, the two servants became a whirlwind of activity, one making the beds and sweeping the floors, the other beginning a feast in the kitchen. That night, I woke up to use the bathroom and discovered I had to go through the servants' quarters to get there. I crept along on tiptoe as quietly as I could, doing my best not to disturb them, but my foot hit something solid, and I tripped. I heard screaming and felt hands grabbing my leg. Somebody turned on the light, and then we were all laughing. The servants had been sleeping on the floor, and I had tripped over them. I wagged my head back and forth, the universal Indian gesture of relationship, did my business, and returned to my room. But before I fell asleep, I realized something:

There was a bed in the other room, and it was empty. Neither of the servants was sleeping in it. *They had chosen to sleep on the floor, next to the empty bed.* They could not conceive of it as their lot in life to sleep in a bed. Gulshan's line whenever Kevin and I picked up our plates from the table flashed into my head: "Cleaning is for us to do."

Every interaction in India was a lesson in the class structure. While munching on masala veggie burgers at the Café Royale near the Regal Cinema in Bombay, I asked Saleem where a college student like him got his spending money. "My parents give it to me," he answered.

"Would you ever do this?" I asked, motioning to the young men dressed in crisp white shirts who were ferrying food back and forth to tables.

Saleem almost choked on his sandwich. "Don't be crazy, boss," he said. "Nobody I know waits tables. Very few people I know in college even have jobs. They all get pocket money from their parents. These people are a different class." He waved his hand in the direction of the waiters and took another bite of his food.

I couldn't help but think that *everybody* I knew in America waited tables or had some other kind of job in their high school and college years. But class worked differently in India. Labor lacked dignity. I thought of an older cousin of mine, Aftab, who had left India for America several years earlier. In India, he was the partying type, constantly shooting pool and riding his motorcycle up and down Bombay's Marine Drive. He was never very interested in education. When he arrived in America, he got a job as an exterminator and worked overtime for almost two years. Then he and a partner bought a convenience store. A year later, he bought his partner out and started looking into another business opportunity, gas stations. He now owns four in West Palm Beach, Florida. In India, none of this would have happened for him because he would never have taken the manual labor job to begin with. Aftab hires recent immigrants and offers the best workers a cut of the business, which gives them the opportunity to climb the ladder the way he did.

My confusion about the separation between the servant class and the upper middle class revealed a quintessentially American point of view. Status is much more fluid in America, at least within the wide range of the population that can loosely be characterized as middle-class. I wait tables at a restaurant, and after my shift is over, I go out to a lounge and someone waits on me. Even if I get a graduate degree and earn a six-figure salary, I don't treat waiters like a permanently lower class. After all, I was one and know what it feels like. And who knows when someone serving me in this restaurant will get their own graduate degree and be my boss. Better to be friendly.

My "American-ness" was starting to stare me in the face in India: not the America of big-screen televisions and Hummers, but the America that, despite its constant failings, managed to inculcate in its citizens a set of humanizing values—the dignity of labor, the fundamental equality of human beings, mobility based on drive and talent, the opportunity to create and contribute.

Someone once told me that the most penetrating exploration of the relationship between identity and nation is found in the writing of James Baldwin. I had brought several books of his essays with me to India, eager to discover in his writing a map for myself. In college, I had looked to black writers for fire. I had identified with their anger and alienation and had carefully crafted an oppositional identity based on their example. Baldwin had walked the same path and had become so consumed by his anger that he left America for Europe to escape the indignity of segregated coffee shops and the brutality of Harlem police officers. But he found that Europe was a stranger to him. When he was mistakenly identified as a thief in Paris and taken to a French jail, he had a morbid wish to be going through the ordeal in the cells of Harlem, where at least he knew how to interpret the facial expressions of the cops. When he met North Africans in the streets of Paris, he realized that they were not his brothers any more than white Parisians were. They did not share his experience of alienation, his anger, or his ache for acceptance. Their mothers had sung them different songs. It was Americans of all walks of life, black intellectuals and white country boys, that Baldwin understood. He followed the logic of this observation and realized that as murderous as America had been to his ancestors, it was the only place that he could call home. Baldwin, like Martin Luther King Jr. and Langston Hughes, made of that surprising fact an opportunity: He started to view himself as a citizen with a stake in the success of America. "I am not a ward of America; I am one of the first Americans to arrive on these shores," he wrote. And he started to realize that the experience of blacks in America had provided them with "a special attitude"—an attitude that had given rise to America's only indigenous expressions, blues and jazz, and some of its most significant heroes, ranging from Frederick Douglass to Harriet Tubman. Black people had been prevented from integrating into American society and had somehow still managed to have a profound impact on the American imagination.

The idea of America was worth fighting for. An experience with an extreme form of an oppositional identity convinced Baldwin of this. He was invited to the home of Elijah Muhammad, the leader of the Nation of Islam. The Nation, Baldwin observed, was not like other angry black organizations in Harlem. White cops didn't rough people up at Nation rallies. They stood in formation at a safe distance, faces set stoically ahead while Nation preachers spoke about the blue-eyed devil, too scared of the intensity and discipline on display to attempt their typical brutality. Elijah Muhammad's ideology was most certainly warped, but Baldwin was impressed by the allegiance it had attracted. Moreover, he was disgusted that white people refused to see the reason for this. After centuries of slavery and subjugation, white Americans were still unable to imagine the anger that seethed within black people. It existed in Baldwin also. He accepted Elijah Muhammad's dinner invitation to determine whether their anger was the same.

The dinner was a regal affair. Nation members, dark and intense, filled the room, the women separated from the men. There was an overwhelming power in Elijah Muhammad's presence. It was time to stop being brainwashed and come to his true self, he told Baldwin. A series of slow, penetrating commands ensued, each followed by a chorus of "Yes, that's right" from the Nation members who surrounded them. Then came the condemnations—of white people, of Christians, of intermarriage, of restaurants where alcohol was served and blacks mingled with whites—all accompanied by the same "Yes, that's right" chorus. Any interaction with the enemy was a denial of the true black self. And then Elijah Muhammad laid out a vision built on this ideology: finding the land to create a black society with a $20 billion economy. In other words, total separation.

The Nation was fast becoming a mass movement with a deeply devoted core of true believers. If Elijah Muhammad made a serious attempt at this goal, tens of thousands might well jump off the cliff with him.

Baldwin understood that this was Elijah Muhammad's response to the racism he had experienced, but his plan was a disaster waiting to happen—not only because it would be impossible to separate people who were so intimately connected economically but also because the plan violated a spiritual principle: namely, human beings were meant to be diverse, and they were meant to live together. America's sin was not just the gross inequality with which the black race had been treated but also its creation of barriers between people. Still, Baldwin felt that there was a chance that America could be redeemed and become a place where people from everywhere collectively created a home. Near the end of *The Fire Next Time*, Baldwin wrote, "If we—and now I mean the relatively conscious whites and the relatively conscious blacks, who must, like lovers, insist on, or create, the consciousness of the others—do not falter in our duty now, we may be able, handful that we are, to end the racial nightmare, and achieve our country, and change the history of the world."

In college, I had understood identity as a box to lock myself in and a bat to bludgeon America with. I was seduced by the notion that we belonged to a tribe based on the identity of our birth, that our loyalty rested exclusively with the tribe, and that one day my tribe of dark-skinned third world people would rise over our white oppressors. I may well have been a candidate for Elijah Muhammad's separate society. But here was James Baldwin, whose ancestors had been enslaved and who knew more about the brutality of white racism than I could ever imagine, saying that love between people of different identities was not only possible but necessary, and that we had to insist on it. Here was a black man who had been chased out of restaurants because he had the temerity to ask for a cup of coffee from the front counter, rejecting separatism in favor of the hope of pluralism, a society where people from different backgrounds worked together, protected one another, sought to achieve something more meaningful for all. Here was a man who viewed identity as a bridge to the possibility of pluralism.

Richard Rodriguez once wrote that Thomas Jefferson, that democrat, was a slaveholder. And Thomas Jefferson, that slaveholder, was a democrat. America embodied that same trauma of contradictions. In college, I had viewed it as my responsibility to expose America's shadow side. But too much emphasis in that direction risked seeing only shadow in the American story and, worse, believing that there was nothing but darkness in its future. That's a cop-out, Baldwin was saying. I realized that it was precisely because of America's glaring imperfections that I should seek to participate in its progress, carve a place in its promise, and play a role in its possibility. And at its heart and at its best, America was about pluralism.

In a strange way, Baldwin's writing on America helped me understand my relationship with India. I relieved India of the burden of being my haven, and I relieved myself of the responsibility of being the reincarnation of Gandhi. My heritage as an Indian in America gave me a special relationship with the country of my citizenship. Why couldn't my citizenship in America provide me with a unique way of relating to the land of my heritage?

My eyes started to adjust. The street scenes that had seemed like nothing but madness two weeks earlier had come into a little more focus. It was not simply random chaos happening on Colaba Causeway, the road that runs between my grandmother's flat and the famous Taj Hotel. It was a thousand carnivals spinning simultaneously and sometimes crashing into one another. There was the carnival of business: ear cleaners, *pan wallas*, single-cigarette dealers, street barbers, sidewalk book merchants. There was the carnival of food: little boys in rags carrying cha and tiffins from office building to office building, sweet meats stacked in display windows, college students lined up outside makeshift *dosa* stands, *kohli* women carrying baskets of fish on their heads and bellowing, "Machi! Machi!" There was the carnival of fashion: young men on motorcycles wearing flared jeans and loose-fitting cotton shirts, young women experimenting with bright styles that mixed India and America, stores advertising bridal outfits and others displaying matching jewelry. There were carnivals of furtive lovers, sidewalk families, street animals, and child beggars. And despite the desperation of so much of life in Bombay, most people seemed happy. They drank tea in cafés, played cards on the sidewalks, bartered playfully in markets, got high on holidays, danced to Hindi music, and dreamed of becoming film stars.

I had picked up enough of the language to have a workable patois of Hindi, English, and hand waving—enough to get me where I was going most of the time. Kevin and I had convinced the servants to teach us how to make chapattis (flat, unleavened breads), which meant they no longer saw us only as lords. It was a far cry from being equals, but it felt much more comfortable to our American minds. We were having a great time with Saleem and Zohra, my two cousins who were only slightly younger than we were. The faculty at their college had conveniently gone on strike during the stretch that Kevin and I were in Bombay, so the two of them and their friends became our social group.

We read for hours every day. We went through stacks of Indian literature: nonfiction by Naipaul, novels by Rushdie, speeches by Vivekananda, poems by Tagore, a history of India by Nehru, various biographies of Gandhi, and, because of our audience with His Holiness, everything we could get our hands on about Tibet, the Dalai

Lama, and Buddhism. We split our time between the carnivals of India outside and the idea of India inside. And the more I immersed myself in Indian civilization, the more I recognized the faint outlines of myself in its vast mirror.

I found myself rejecting Naipaul's cold, exacting pessimism of India—that it was a million mutinies and an area of darkness. Somehow, amid its poverty and filth, India danced. Naipaul seemed incapable of seeing that joy as anything but an opiate. Perhaps he had no rhythm.

I was drawn to the hopefulness expressed by other Indian writers, to their visions of what India could be, what it was meant to be. I loved their ability to weave the worlds of ancient religious texts and village life and the Mughal Empire into a garment of possibility. Here was Rushdie's protagonist in *Midnight's Children*, Saleem Sinai, hosting conferences of the children born at the moment of India's liberation —Hindus and Muslims and Sikhs; the sons of beggars and the daughters of successful businessmen—each of them holding forth on what her country's identity should be. The evil work of the antagonist of the novel, Shiva, was to destroy the dialogue.

Indeed, the common theme that ran through these hopeful visions was India as a civilization whose diverse communities were in deep dialogue with one another. The emperor Ashoka, who, more than two thousand years ago, managed both to spread Buddhism and to encourage interfaith discussions, said, "Other sects should be duly honored in every way on all occasions." The sixteenth-century Muslim emperor Akbar invited leaders and scholars from all of India's various religions to debate one another in his court, scenes of which are depicted in paintings that have come to be considered characteristic of Indian art. For centuries, persecuted religious communities—Parsees, Tibetan Buddhists, Jews, and Baha'is—have found India's doors open to them. The great poet and contemporary of Gandhi, Rabindranath Tagore, wrote that the "idea of India" itself militates "against the intense consciousness of the separateness of one's own people from others."

The dream of India is the dream of pluralism, the idea of different communities retaining their uniqueness while relating in a way that recognizes they share universal values. It is a dream I recognized from the writings of James Baldwin. It is the American dream also. And just as America has sinned against its dream with slavery and racism, India has violated its promise with religious nationalism.

It was a sin my family knew well. In January 1993, the Hindu nationalist Shiv Sena organized groups of saffron-clad thugs to terrorize the Muslim population of Bombay. My cousin Saleem saw one of these groups armed with machetes pull down the pants of a little boy. Saleem turned and ran as fast as he could, but he still heard the scream. His parents had told him about these murders. Chanting Hindu nationalist slogans, the Shiv Sena marauders surrounded young boys and pulled their pants down. If they were circumcised, it meant they were Muslim, which meant they were dead.

For Saleem's parents, my aunt and uncle, this was the final straw. They locked themselves in their apartments, taking their nameplates, which marked them as Muslims, off their mailboxes so that the roaming mobs would not know who lived there. They lived that way for several weeks, not going to work or school, afraid for their lives, afraid of their city.

In 1998, the year I returned to India, the BJP, a Hindu nationalist political party, was elected into national office. They had whipped up a frenzy of support from certain Hindu groups by stating that, centuries earlier, a Muslim emperor had destroyed a Hindu temple, which they claimed was the birthplace of a Hindu god, and had built a mosque over the rubble. The second in command of the BJP had led a campaign to destroy the mosque, a move that many Hindus in India saw as both patriotic and faithful, the very definition of religious nationalism.

I remember one of my aunts expressing dismay and concern over the election: "This is bad for Muslims; it is bad for Hindus; it is bad for India." I don't think even she knew how bad. Under the BJP, India exploded a nuclear bomb, the "Hindu bomb" it was called. Pakistan followed with its own nuclear test. Tensions between the two nations, which had fought three wars in the past half century, rose dramatically. That made life more difficult for Muslims in India. Although India has just about as many Muslims, 130 million, as Pakistan, the Hindu nationalist rhetoric coming from the government constantly questioned their loyalty to the nation.

The BJP's allies started weaving Hindu nationalism into the fabric of Indian life. They changed textbooks to teach the Hindu nationalist line. Muslims found it harder to get certain jobs. Police forces, some very much in the control of Hindu nationalist elements, became more brazen in their brutality toward Muslims. A few years later, in 2002, Hindu nationalist groups in Gujarat, a state run by a strong BJP ally, went on a murder spree that took the lives of about two thousand Muslims. In some places, the police force stood by and watched. In others, it actively aided and abetted the murder. Almost no one has been prosecuted. The governor of the state, Narendra Modi, won his reelection campaign later that year.

Gandhi, a devout Hindu, had long maintained that Hindu-Muslim unity was just as important to him as a free India. His murderer was a member of a Hindu nationalist organization, the RSS. In the fury and sadness that followed the assassination of the father of the nation, the articulator of its dream of freedom and pluralism, the Hindu nationalists went underground. But they returned with a vengeance in the 1990s, and it was not just Muslims that they were targeting, but the very idea of India itself.

One of the proudest moments in India's recent history was its granting refuge to the Dalai Lama when he was forced to flee Chinese occupation of his native Tibet. Buddhism was founded in India but had nearly disappeared over the centuries. The Dalai Lama brought it back. He set up his government in exile in Dharamsala, a small city in the foothills of the Himalayas which attracted an eclectic mix of old Tibetan monks and young Western seekers. It was here that Kevin and I traveled for our audience with His Holiness.

What do you say to the Dalai Lama when you are with him? It is a question worthy of a Zen koan. We met with His Holiness in the visiting room of his small palace. He presented us with the traditional Tibetan white scarves and said he had heard of us from Brother Wayne. We spent a moment drinking in his presence with our eyes.

His Holiness was in a playful mood. He reached out and put his index finger on the chain that Kevin was wearing around his neck, a string of beads with a small bowl on the end, given to him by a Native American couple at the United Religions Initiative conference. "Emptiness," the Dalai Lama said. "I like it." And then he giggled.

"I spent many years studying the concept of emptiness in Buddhism," Kevin explained. "Ultimately, it brought me back to a similar notion in Judaism—the idea of ayin, which means that God was once the entirety of creation, and the universe as we know it was brought about when God contracted Himself. That contraction caused a shattering of light across the world, and we human beings are carriers of that light."

The Dalai Lama listened intently and nodded. "Yes," he said, "this is a very spiritual concept. You are a Jew?"

"Yes," Kevin said. He finally felt comfortable embracing that identity. He still practiced Buddhist meditation and read widely in other religions, but it was clear that his roots were in Judaism. Somehow, the things Brother Wayne had told us—that studying other religions should first and foremost have the effect of strengthening our understanding of our own—had sunk in for Kevin. More and more, I saw Kevin with his nose in a book about Judaism. He would constantly tell me about Jewish spirituality and social justice theology, comparing Jewish concepts to ideas in other religions. He always ended with a diatribe against the Hebrew school he had gone to when he was younger: "Why didn't my rabbi teach us this stuff? All he ever talked about was rituals and Jewish chosenness, never Jewish social justice."

The Dalai Lama seemed happy. "Judaism is a very good religion," he said. "I have many Jewish friends. We have interfaith dialogue. I learn a lot from them. Judaism and Buddhism are very much alike. You should learn more about both and become a better Jew." I have never seen Kevin look happier. The Dalai Lama reached over and touched the beads around his neck again and then rubbed his head and laughed.

Then he turned to me. I started getting a little nervous. I knew what was coming. The Dalai Lama was about to ask me about my religion. He had just commended Kevin for deepening his Jewish identity. Somehow I didn't think he was going to be impressed with my story of trying to be a Buddhist. Yet try as I might, I just could not get the hang of it. I had a little secret that I hadn't even told Kevin: I was a total failure at Buddhist meditation. Our version of it was to sit cross-legged and quietly focus on nothingness. By the time I got my legs in order and my back straight and I took my first full breath, a thought would enter my mind. I would try to shove it out. But halfway through my next breath, another thought would penetrate. I spent the whole time I was meditating shoving thoughts out of my head and being mad at myself for being a bad Buddhist. Those thoughts were my greatest enemy. My Western materialist upbringing was preventing me from entering the original mind.

Lately, though, I had gotten tired of shoving thoughts out of my head, and I had allowed one to linger long enough to get a sense of what it was. I could not have been more shocked at the discovery: "Ya Ali, Ya Muhammad"—the prayer that my mother had taught me when I was a child, the prayer that was meant to help me fall asleep and keep me safe through the night. The realization startled me. It had been such a long time since I had said that prayer intentionally, but here it was floating in my head, still woven into my being. I decided to let it stay, even if it didn't abide by the rules we had made up and called Buddhist meditation. I knew my intention was pure, even if I wasn't skilled at creating and focusing on nothingness.

But after hearing the Dalai Lama and Kevin talk about Judaism and Buddhism, I started forming a different theory about my Buddhist meditation. Maybe, as Kevin's study of Buddhist concepts had helped him understand Jewish concepts, my novice foray into Buddhist meditation had inadvertently returned me to Muslim prayer. The Ismailis are a spiritualist Muslim community with an emphasis on meditation, and one of our techniques is to focus the mind on a particular Muslim prayer word or phrase. Perhaps Buddhist meditation had brought the Muslim spirituality from deep within me to the surface. Perhaps this was God's gentle way of telling me something.

When the Dalai Lama opened his mouth, it wasn't to ask a question; it was to make a statement. "You are a Muslim," he said. Brother Wayne must have told him. Or maybe the Dalai Lama's brother, with whom we were staying in Dharamsala. Or, really, who knows how the Dalai Lama found out. I imagine Dalai Lamas know some things that the rest of us don't.

"You are a Muslim," the Dalai Lama repeated.

"Yes," I said, then swallowed. The Dalai Lama giggled. "Islam is a very good religion. Buddhists and Muslims lived in peace in Tibet for many centuries. First, there were only Tibetan Buddhists. Now there are Tibetan Muslims, too. You should visit them."

Kevin and I spent a few minutes talking about the Interfaith Youth Corps, how it hoped to bring young people from different religions together to serve others.

"This is very important," the Dalai Lama said, suddenly growing serious. "Religions must dialogue, but even more, they must come together to serve others. Service is the most important. And common values, finding common values between different religions. And as you study the other religions, you must learn more about your own and believe more in your own. This Interfaith Youth Corps is a very good project."

And then he turned slightly to face Kevin and me together. "Jew," he said, and pointed at Kevin. "Muslim," he said, and pointed at me. "Buddhists," he said, and pointed at himself and his secretary. "This is interfaith. Now we have to serve others. But we"—the Dalai Lama pointed to his secretary and himself—"are not young. Can we still join?"

He sent us away laughing and floating and believing.

In *The Jew in the Lotus*, Rodger Kamenetz writes that many young people view religion as an old man saying no. Growing up, my "old man"
was a woman—my grandmother, with whom I was now staying in
Bombay. She would come to the States every few years and live with
my family, occupying the living room from midmorning to early
evening watching Hindi films. I avoided her as much as possible. "Are
you saying your Du'a?" she would ask if she caught me before I managed to reach the back staircase. If she woke up earlier than usual and
saw me at the breakfast table before I left for school, she would say,
"Are you giving your *dasond?*" referring to the tithe that Ismailis give.
She was disappointed that I had no close Ismaili friends when I was a
teenager. "You will marry an Ismaili, right?" my grandmother would
ask, catching my arm, as I was sneaking out. I am embarrassed to say
it now, but I dreaded her visits and did my best to avoid her.

My view of her changed dramatically on this trip to India. She
spent most of her days sitting on a simple sofa bed in the living room,
clad in white, tasbih in hand, beads flowing through her fingers, whispering the name of God—"Allah, Allah, Allah"—over and over. She
would cry during prayer, the name of the Prophet causing an overflow
of love from deep in her heart. I told her all about the Dalai Lama, my
voice filled with admiration. I am sure she wished that I spoke as excitedly about the Aga Khan, but she never said as much. Instead, she
asked me to read stories about His Holiness to her and observed, "All
great religious leaders are alike."

She loved Kevin. Every morning, when Kevin and I were reading
in our room, she would bellow for him from across the apartment: "*Ke-
vaauuun!*" He would get out of his chair, pad across the living room,
and put his head in Mama's lap, and she would stroke it and whisper
Arabic prayers over him, asking God to keep him safe and on the
straight path. When we first arrived, she saw Kevin's books on Judaism and asked, "You are a Jew?" Kevin nodded. "Masha'Allah," my
grandmother said, meaning "Thanks be to God." Then she turned to

me and said, "He is Ahl al-Kitab." Muslims use this term, meaning "a person of the book," to refer to their Abrahamic cousins, Jews and Christians.

Earlier in her life, it seemed as though my grandmother could speak to me about nothing but Islam, but now she rarely brought it up at all. Yet, through her interest in Buddhism, her constant Zikr (the Muslim term for remembrance of God through prayer), and her love for Kevin, I was getting a sense of what it meant to be a Muslim.

The most important lesson came in the most unexpected way. I woke up one morning to find a new woman in the apartment. She looked a little scared and disheveled, and she was wearing a torn white nightgown several sizes too big for her, probably one of my grandmother's older outfits. She didn't appear to be a new servant or a family friend.

"Who is she?" I asked my grandmother.

"I don't know her real name. The leader of the prayer house brought her here. She is getting abused at home by her father and uncle. We will take care of her until we can find somewhere safe to send her. We will call her Anisa."

I turned to look at Anisa, who was sitting on the floor with a plate of dal and rice in front of her. She returned my gaze, a little more confident than before. She looked as if she was easing into her new surroundings.

I turned back to my grandmother and said, "Mama, what if these crazy men, this father and uncle, come looking for her? Do you think it's safe to keep this woman here? I mean, Kevin and I are here now, but when we're gone, who will protect you and the servants if they come around?"

My grandmother looked at me a bit suspiciously, as if to say that she had little hope for protection from us. "We will check the door before we answer it. And God is with us," she said.

I couldn't restrain myself. "Mama, this is crazy. You can't just take strange women into your home and keep them here for weeks or months. This isn't the Underground Railroad, you know. You're old now. This is dangerous."

"Crazy, huh?" she responded. "How old are you?"

"Twenty-two."

"I have been doing this for forty-five years. That's more than twice as long as you've been on earth. This may be the fiftieth, sixtieth, hundredth person who has come here and been safe." She got up and walked slowly over to the cabinet and took down a box. "Come here," she told me. She lifted the lid, and I looked inside and saw a mess of Polaroids. "I took pictures of them." She reached into the box and picked up a picture. "This one was so pretty. Her father was an alcoholic. Her mother died in a car accident. She was afraid that he would sell her into prostitution for money to drink. Some friends told her about me—Ashraf Ma-ji, they would call me—and she saved up some money, a rupee here and there from small sewing jobs, until she had enough for the train from Ahmedabad. It was the middle of the monsoon season. She was dripping wet when she came to the door. Barely seventeen. So scared, so beautiful. She didn't talk for two weeks. But slowly, slowly she came around. We sent her to school to improve her sewing, and we found her a good husband. She lives in Hyderabad now. She has had two children and started a very successful sewing business."

My grandmother started going through the other Polaroids. There was a poor woman with three young sons from the south of India who had heard about my grandmother and come for help. A woman from Calcutta who could neither hear nor speak and whose parents had abandoned her. Several girls whose fathers were sexually and physically abusive. My grandmother helped them find jobs or husbands, sent them back to school, or helped them locate family members in other parts of India. She had made little notes on the back of each Polaroid: name, birthday, current address. The more stories she told about the people she had saved, the more I realized how little I knew about my grandmother.

"Why do you do this?" I finally blurted out.

She looked a little shocked that I would ask, as if to say that the answer was self-evident. But just in case it wasn't clear to me, she said simply, "I am a Muslim. This is what Muslims do."

6

The Story of Islam,
the Story of Pluralism

> *I can only answer the question "What am I to do?"*
> *if I can answer the prior question "Of what story*
> *or stories do I find myself a part?"*
> ALASDAIR MACINTYRE

I knew perfectly well that it was dumb luck that I was heading across
the ocean on Cecil Rhodes's money in September 1998. My biggest
concern was that I was going to be found out. My peculiar charm
might have gotten me this far, but I knew it had no hope of working
in England, land of stiff lips, dry humor, and endlessly wet days. It
would most certainly fail to impress my fellow Rhodes scholars, who I
was convinced were all budding Nobel laureates and Harvard faculty.

    My first few months at Oxford confirmed all my fears. The other
Rhodes scholars all seemed to speak multiple languages and be on
a first-name basis with their home state senators. They spoke confi-
dently about their careers—Yale Law School, a U.S. Supreme Court
clerkship, a few years making bank in the corporate world and then a
turn to politics, which would probably end in being a state governor.
If they chose to stick with the law, they had their eyes set on the fed-

eral bench. I was astounded at their absolute conviction that they were meant for global leadership. When a student arrived at the University of Illinois, people talked about how far the Fighting Illini might go in the NCAA tournament that season. Apparently, the messages were different at the fancy private schools where so many Rhodes scholars had been educated. There, it seemed, people were crawling about whispering in undergraduates' ears that the world was just waiting for them to take over.

Somehow, all my fears coalesced around *The New Yorker*. It was the magazine I most often saw the other Rhodes scholars reading. I had never even heard of it before I arrived at Oxford. At the University of Illinois, reading the *Chicago Tribune* made you more knowledgeable about world affairs than just about anybody else. Every week for the first few months I was at Oxford, I went to the newsstand on Little Clarendon Street and bought *The New Yorker*. Then I walked back through the rain to my coffin-size room and stared at it. That only seemed to heighten my anxiety. I couldn't even decipher the damn cover; how was I supposed to understand the articles?

I was tempted to tell myself the story that middle-class midwestern kids like me were all about keeping it real and that the Ivy League snobs I had been shipped here with were so full of a sickening sense of entitlement that they weren't even worth talking to. But I knew that was a lie born of fear and prejudice. Moreover, it undermined the whole reason I had applied for a Rhodes in the first place. If I was going to dismiss my fellow Rhodes scholars so easily, I might as well have stayed home.

Self-righteousness and feelings of inadequacy are close cousins. Once I admitted to myself that winning a Rhodes was a fluke and that everyone around me was smarter and more deserving, I figured the only thing I could do was accept my luck as God's grace and try to make the most of the experience. I joined a reading group that met at Holywell Manor, a residence for graduate students near the center of Oxford. We read mostly twentieth-century work—Jhumpa Lahiri,

Philip Roth, Vikram Seth, Zora Neale Hurston—and talked about the books in relation to the issues around us. I was determined to absorb the erudition of the other Rhodes scholars. Whenever someone mentioned a philosopher I had never heard of, I looked up his or her articles. When a topic was raised that I was unfamiliar with, I went out and bought a stack of books on it. And I finally stopped trying to figure out the cover of *The New Yorker* and started to read the articles.

Professor Geoffrey Walford was not my idea of an Oxford don. There was no pipe in his mouth, and he did not walk around in black robes. He was rail thin, wore blue jeans every day, insisted on his students calling him Geoffrey, and, unlike many professors, was totally committed to helping me both to complete a quality dissertation and have a good experience in graduate school. I remember my first meeting with him. He had his glasses on and my file open on his desk. "American," he said, and looked up. I nodded.

"Rhodes scholar," he continued. I was hoping that would impress him. Something about his arched eyebrows told me that getting impressed wasn't really his thing.

"I've supervised other American Rhodes scholars," he told me. "The problem with your type is that you tire of libraries and computers quite quickly. You are always off trying to *do* something, being involved in 'the world's fight' I believe you call it. Whatever you want to do is fine with me really. Let's just make sure you don't waste your time here. You should get a doctorate in a topic that will actually hold your interest and ideally connect with your career. That means one thing if you want to be an academic and another thing if you are going in a different direction."

I couldn't believe my ears. The biggest horror story I'd heard from friends of mine in doctoral programs was that their professors thought the academic life was the only life worth living. Too often, graduate school is like one long hazing experience intended to turn you into a clone of your academic adviser. Yet here was a professor, a don at Oxford no less, basically encouraging me down a career path of social change and offering to help me get a doctorate on a topic that interested me on the way.

"Well, the thing I've been thinking about most is the relationship between religious identity and interfaith cooperation," I said. Geoffrey listened with interest. His own current research was on the growth of faith-based schools, both Muslim and Christian, in Europe. As a qualitative sociologist, he had spent a significant amount of time as a participant-observer in these schools and interviewed several key players. He suggested identifying an educational space that nurtured both religious identity and encouraged interfaith relations. And, because the Department of Educational Studies at Oxford was working in partnership with several Ismaili institutions, Geoffrey knew about the recent developments in Ismaili religious education. He suggested that I explore those.

The first time I met Azim Nanji, I got the sense that he was a man who would play a key role in my life. A well-regarded professor of Islamic studies who had chaired the Department of Religion at the University of Florida, Azim had recently been appointed by the Ismaili Imam as the director of the Institute of Ismaili Studies in London. I went to see him in the fall of my first year at Oxford and told him that I was interested in doing a doctorate on Ismaili religious education programs. He nodded his approval. Ismaili religious education had gone through a profound change over the past two decades, transforming from a casual affair that essentially imparted the rites and ceremonies of one ethnic group of Ismailis into an intellectually challenging, broad-ranging program that explored the history, aesthetics, and ethics of Islam. Azim and the Institute of Ismaili Studies had been at the center of this transformation.

But Azim knew that I was interested in something more significant than a doctorate. I was embarking on an intensely personal journey. The perspective I brought to Islam had been shaped by my admiration for Dorothy Day, Mahatma Gandhi, and the Dalai Lama, as well as my friendships with Kevin and Brother Wayne. I loved the spirituality and social justice in Christianity, Hinduism, Judaism, and Buddhism. I had had no interest in Islam until my most recent trip to India, when I had found Muslim prayer surfacing in my Buddhist meditation, when the Dalai Lama had told me to be a good Muslim, and when I had seen my grandmother model what that meant. Now I wanted to learn about the tradition behind her spiritual equanimity and service ethic. Were there heroes in my faith like Abraham Joshua Heschel and Martin Luther King Jr.? Did it have poets like Tagore and Blake? Philosophers like Maimonides and Aquinas? Had my faith helped free countries the way that Gandhi's Hinduism had? Did it have mouth-widening beauty, like the Sistine Chapel? I knew nothing of Islam except that it lived in my bones. I desperately wanted it to be magnificent.

Without my explaining any of this directly, Azim somehow understood that this was the animating impulse behind my dissertation topic. He looked at me intently as I explained what I wanted to research, then said, "So many of us begin our careers by studying our history and then locating ourselves within it. My own dissertation was in a similar area. You are living at a time when Islam can go in many different directions, and it will be young people like you who are shaping its next steps. Having an understanding of the humanistic dimensions of Muslim history and how to teach them most effectively is about as important an education as you can get. I want you to know that my door is always open to you."

The early influences on our religious path make all the difference. That truism is shockingly illustrated by the example of Yusuf Islam.

When I was a child, my father and I spent a lot of our time together listening to music. For my tenth birthday, he got me *Led Zeppelin II* and *Stop Making Sense* by the Talking Heads. About that time, he started taking me to concerts. I remember singing along to "Gypsy" by the Moody Blues and chanting with the crowd for the Kinks to do an encore. I learned to love live music. Whenever my dad put on a new record, I would ask if we could go see the musician play. Often he would tell me that the band had broken up because one of the members had died, as in the case of John Bonham and Led Zeppelin or Jim Morrison and the Doors. But I never quite understood his explanation for why we couldn't go see Cat Stevens, my favorite singer-songwriter.

"He's not dead, right?" I'd ask my dad.

"No, he's alive," my dad would say, a bit of frustration creeping into his voice.

"So why doesn't he tour anymore?"

"He became a Muslim—a rigid Muslim, who thinks music is against the religion," my dad would answer, unable to mask his anger.

I was confused. We were Muslims, too, and we liked music. Even more, I thought that the most spiritual music I had ever heard— "Peace Train," "Moonshadow," "Wild World," "Father and Son"— had come from this guy with the funny name. It was only much later that I learned the whole story.

When Cat Stevens, now Yusuf Islam, converted to Islam in the late 1970s, he happened to fall in with a group of Muslims who told him that music was against his new faith. This was an entirely legitimate interpretation of Islam, but very much on the severe end, and a damn shame considering the gift that God had given him. It wasn't until the early 1990s that Yusuf came under a different influence and rethought his position on music.

It was the time of the Balkans war, and Yusuf, like most Muslims and many other citizens of good faith around the world, watched as the Bosnians were murdered en masse by the Serbs while the United States, Britain, France, and others barely lifted a finger. He found himself growing angrier and angrier and feeling more and more helpless. One day, he got a phone call from a Bosnian aid agency. "Do something for the children being killed here," the person on the other end of the line said. "Organize an international concert—use your talent."

Yusuf was torn. He had been told by an earlier influence that music was un-Islamic, but here was a group of Muslims asking for his help in the form of his gift—music. A few weeks later, Yusuf was visited by the Bosnian foreign minister, Irfan Ljubijankic, a Muslim and a doctor who had heroically saved the lives of many Bosnians in the basement of his home using the crudest medical instruments.

As a young man, Dr. Ljubijankic had been deeply inspired by Cat Stevens's music, so much so that he had started playing music himself. When they met, Dr. Ljubijankic put in a cassette with a song he had written, "I Have No Cannons That Roar." Yusuf was deeply moved by the song. Dr. Ljubijankic placed the cassette in his hand and said, "Please use it if you can for helping the cause."

Some time later, the doctor's helicopter was shot down over Bihac, and he died. Yusuf played the cassette the doctor had given him over and over. He also started listening to other music coming out of Bosnia—hymns and songs called *nashids*, which were providing the Bosnians with an enormous amount of inspiration during the war. Listening to these songs, Yusuf had a sudden realization: "Here was a magnificently potent tool; we simply had to use it."

Yusuf, wishing to remain true to his faith and also provide his gift of music to the Bosnians, started studying with other teachers and returned to the traditions of Islam to explore further the permissibility of music. He found that the Prophet allowed and even encouraged music when it served a positive end. He was surprised that the Muslims who had told him that music was against Islam had not pointed out this crucial distinction. One line in his essay "Islam Sings" articulates a central truism in the formation of every individual's religious identity: "It's interesting to note now how my formative years as a Muslim were shaped by those I came into contact with."

Yusuf Islam started to make music again.

Azim Nanji's understanding of Islam can be summed up in the famous saying of the Prophet Muhammad: "God is beautiful and loves beauty." I would stop in to see Azim about once a month. He had usually just returned from, or was about to leave for, a trip abroad—lecturing at Aga Khan University in Pakistan, visiting early childhood educational programs in East Africa, attending the ceremony for the

Aga Khan Award for Architecture in Syria, meeting with the Imam in Paris. Even so, our time together always felt relaxed. "How did Islam, a faith with such a highly focused monotheism, find a place in Hindu India, with its millions of Gods?" I asked. And Azim told me a story. Once, there was a Sufi sheikh who came with his followers to the state of Gujarat in India. He sent word to the local Hindu prince that he had arrived and wanted to stay. The Hindu prince sent a servant with a full glass of milk to the sheikh, as if to say, "We are already complete here." The sheikh mixed in a spoonful of sugar and sent the sweetened milk back to the prince, as if to say, "My people and I will only contribute positively to this community."

"I love spiritual poetry," I once told Azim. "Blake and Tagore and Whitman. I feel like every nation and religion has a few shining souls who give utterance to the values of their tradition in a way that makes them seem both unique and universal."

"Ah, yes," Azim responded. "I love those poets, too. But my favorite spiritual poet is Rumi, a Muslim born in Afghanistan in the thirteenth century." I almost fell off my chair. Of course I had heard of Rumi. I had seen dozens of his volumes on bookstore shelves. But he was a Muslim? I had no idea. "Some people call Rumi's great opus, *The Mathnawi*, 'the Qur'an in the Persian tongue,'" Azim continued. He told me Rumi's story, how he had been a scholar of Islamic law, making legal rulings and giving stern lectures, until a man in rags approached him one day. "What's this?" the man asked Rumi, pointing to his law books.

"You wouldn't understand," Rumi responded disdainfully.

The man fixed Rumi in a steely gaze, waved his arm, and set the books on fire. Then he waved his arm again, and the books appeared unharmed.

"What was that?" Rumi asked, shocked.

"You wouldn't understand," he said, and disappeared. The man was Shams of Tabriz, and in that moment Rumi made the decision to give up his law books and follow the mystical path of love and spirituality that Shams embodied—the Sufi path.

I almost couldn't restrain myself. I wanted to be reading Rumi right there, right then. Azim smiled and started reciting some of his favorite Rumi lines:

> I am not from east or west
> not up from the ground
> or out of the ocean
> my place is placeless
> a trace of the traceless
> I belong to the beloved

I told Azim about my grandmother in Bombay and how she sheltered women and children in her home. "Oh, yes, Ashraf Ma-ji," Azim said.

"You've heard of her?" I asked, incredulous.

"Of course. She is one of the living saints of the Ismaili tradition. Your family," Azim said, leaning in a little closer, "has lived the service ethic of Islam as well as any that I have known. Your grandmother's father started the Ismaili Volunteer Corps. Your grandfather Major Ebrahim Patel was one of the key pillars of the Ismaili community in India and very close to the Imam. Your aunt in Bombay was the first female president of a major Ismaili national council. Your uncle in Nairobi was the Imam's ambassador to the Kenyan government for many years. Yes, it seems that Islam's service ethic is being passed down the generations in your family. I wonder what you will do with it?"

"Where does this service ethic come from?" I asked.

"From God, at the moment of creation," Azim said. I looked at him a little blankly.

"It is best articulated in Sura 2 of the Holy Qur'an," he told me.

I went home, opened my English translation of the Qur'an, and read. God created Adam, the first human and therefore the representative of all humankind, by blowing His breath into a lump of clay. God made Adam His *abd* (servant) and *khalifa* (representative on earth). It was Adam's responsibility to be a good steward of God's beautiful creation, taking care of the oceans and rivers, the forests and animals. After God deputized Adam, He called the angels forth and told them to offer respect to His vicegerent on earth. But the angels refused and responded, "Will You put there a being who will work mischief on the earth and shed blood, while we sing Your glories and exalt Your utter holiness?" God did not refute the angels directly, instead choosing to say, "I know what you do not know." God then set up a contest between Adam and the angels, asking each to name the different parts of creation. The Angels could not do it, protesting that the only knowledge they possessed was for glorifying God's name. God turned to Adam, who proceeded to accomplish the task.

I finished the story, closed the Qur'an, touched it to my forehead, and kissed it. Outside, the grass in Oxford, greener than anything I had seen before, seemed as if it was shining and pointing to heaven. Two blue-winged birds flew out of one of Oxford's towering trees into the hedges below, cawing loudly. I saw a boy and his mother walking, finished with their afternoon play, going home for dinner. She playfully grabbed the ball from him and began to run away with it. He laughed and followed her. This was creation. God had made it holy, had entrusted humanity to be His representative here. From the time of our ancestor Adam, each human had been given God's breath, a great goodness that not even the angels could perceive but that God knew and spoke of. And what were we able to do that the angels could not, that gave us the ability to serve as stewards of creation? We could name things. We had creativity. We could learn and apply our learning to improve creation. And suddenly I understood my grandmother in India much better. And Dorothy Day and King and Heschel and Gandhi and the Dalai Lama. I felt as if I had a glimpse into their goodness, as if I knew something more of their Source.

The sun was almost finished setting. I remember my mother referring to this as Maghrib time, the holy moment when it is both night and day on earth. Prayer time. I went to my knees, touched my forehead and nose to the floor in sijda, and came back up—the same motion that the angels made when they saw the Prophet Muhammad ascending through the heavens to meet with God. I cupped my hands, closed my eyes, and started reciting Sura al-Fatiha, the first chapter of the Holy Qur'an: "Bismillah Ar Rahman Ar Rahim. Alhamdolillah Ar Rabbil Al Amin." It had been years since I had said it. But somehow, it came back to me, came pouring from my heart onto my lips and out into the world, as if carried on the breath of God.

Under the guidance of Azim Nanji, I learned that Islam is best understood not as a set of rigid rules and a list of required rituals but as a story that began with Adam and continues through us; as a tradition of prophets and poets who raised great civilizations by seeking to give expression to the fundamental ethos of the faith.

I found the clearest articulation of that fundamental ethos in the writing of Fazlur Rahman, a professor at the University of Chicago until his death in 1988. One of the most influential Muslim minds of the twentieth century, Rahman emphasized that the core message of Islam is the establishment of an ethical, egalitarian order on earth. He insisted that all the passages of the Qur'an be read in that general light. The central aspect of this moral order is merciful justice, embodied first and foremost in Allah—the Arabic term for "the God," signaling that there are no others—and then in the prophets that He sends to earth with guidance. God also gives each human an inner light, which the Qur'an refers to as *taqwa*, the writing of God on our souls. Rahman called taqwa the single most important concept in the Qur'an. It is the piece of us that innately knows the mercy of God. And God, as it says in the Qur'an, sent Muhammad and his followers to be nothing but a special mercy upon all the worlds.

I read biographies of Muhammad. He came of age during a time that Muslims now refer to as *jahilliya* (a period of darkness), when the lesson of monotheism and mercy that had begun with Adam and had continued through his successors—Noah, Abraham, Moses, and Jesus—had been replaced by a rampant materialism and a worship of false idols. Muhammad became a well-respected merchant in Mecca, often asked by his fellow Arabs to mediate disputes. Every year, he made a retreat to Mount Hira, where he would pray, fast, and give alms to the poor. During his retreat in the year 610, Muhammad felt a powerful force envelop him and heard this command: "Iqra" (Recite). Though illiterate, Muhammad found the first revelation of the Holy Qur'an pouring from his mouth: "Recite in the name of your Lord who created." Some traditions say that Muhammad was frightened and confused by this incident, thinking that perhaps a demon had possessed him. He ran back to his wife, a well-regarded businesswoman named Khadija, and she assured him that God would not let a demon enter a man as pious and righteous as he. She took Muhammad to see her cousin, Waraqa, a Christian. Waraqa listened carefully to the story, looked deep into Muhammad's eyes and forehead (where the light of God is said to reveal itself), and declared to Khadija that the prophecy had come true: God's messenger to the Arabs had arrived. Waraqa and Khadija, a Christian and a woman, were the first people to recognize Muhammad's prophetic call. For the next twenty-three years, Muhammad guided a growing community of converts in the religion that became called Islam (the term means "submission to the will of God," and its followers became known as Muslims), a faith that Muhammad repeatedly stated was not new but simply a return to God's original message of monotheism and mercy.

I studied the great medieval caliphates of Islam. The Abbassids in Baghdad, who discovered Aristotle and translated his work from Greek to Arabic. The Umayyads in Córdoba, considered the most learned city in Europe at its peak, referred to even by European Christians as "the ornament of the world." The Fatimids in Cairo, an Ismaili empire that built the great Muslim seat of learning, Al Azhar, along with hundreds of libraries and other centers of scholarship. I marveled at the pluralism that Muslim empires had nurtured and protected. The Mughal emperor Akbar was hosting interfaith dialogues in sixteenth-century India while religious wars raged in Europe.

I learned about the role that Muslims had played in modern freedom movements. That Abdul Ghaffar Khan (also known as Badshah

Khan), a Pashtun Muslim (coming from the same tribe as Afghanistan's Taliban), played a key part alongside Gandhi in liberating India from British rule, guided by his interpretation of Islam as a nonviolent tradition of liberation. I read Farid Esack's *Qur'an, Liberation and Pluralism* on the central role of Muslims in the struggle against apartheid in South Africa.

I saw the ethos of Islam brightly expressed in the work of the Aga Khan Development Network (AKDN), the development institutions established by the Aga Khan, the Ismaili Imam. In forgotten parts of the world such as Central Asia and West Africa, the AKDN is providing microloans to villagers to start small businesses and establishing integrated systems of education and health care. The AKDN is building the first university in Central Asia and is expanding Aga Khan University in Karachi, one of the best institution of higher education in the Muslim world, to include a campus in East Africa. It is investing in projects that protect Islam's vibrant cultural heritage of architecture, calligraphy, and music. The AKDN includes one of the most respected disaster relief organizations in the world, Focus. When a horrible earthquake struck Kashmir in 2005, the Pakistani government relied on AKDN helicopters to get help to the region. Over and over, the Imam has emphasized that the AKDN is a modern expression of the Islamic ethos of dignity, service, and beauty. In other words, the Aga Khan is much more than a philanthropist; he is a Muslim.

I watched myself effortlessly making each leap of faith—that there is one God; that He chose humanity as His vicegerent on earth with the purpose of creating a moral social order; that He sent messengers with guidance for this world; that the final Prophet was a merchant named Muhammad, who received the message we call the Holy Qur'an through the angel Gabriel; that Islam was such a rich tradition that it had given rise to many *tariqas* (spiritual paths) and *madhabs* (schools of thought), one of them being the Ismaili tariqa, which stated that God would provide humanity with a leader who would give guidance in how to interpret the Qur'anic message to meet the challenges of each new era. I learned the Ismaili Du'a again in full. I went to the Oxford Centre for Islamic Studies and had someone teach me the salat prayer that most Muslims do five times a day. I started to fast during Ramadan.

As I had come to terms with my brown skin, with my Indian heritage, with my American citizenship, I realized that I was now facing and understanding the part of myself that was both first and final: I was a Muslim.

Faith, wrote the great scholar Wilfred Cantwell Smith, is the way a believer connects with a religious tradition. A tradition, wrote the poet T. S. Eliot, is not simply inherited; it is something acquired only by great labor. It was the ethic of service and pluralism in Islam that I felt most enlivened by and most responsible to. Starting the Interfaith Youth Corps gave me the chance to put that ethic into action, to feel worthy of the designation "Muslim."

With the help of several established interfaith organizations, I gathered a group of sixteen young people from four continents and six different religions to discuss the basic principles of the Interfaith Youth Corps in the Bay Area in June 1999. The conference facilitator was Anastasia White, a PhD student in organizational design and a veteran of the reconciliation process in post-apartheid South Africa. She pushed us to view the Interfaith Youth Corps as more a movement than a project. I thought about the movements I had admired during my college years—the Catholic Worker, service learning, multiculturalism. Each one had a core idea that ignited passion across a broad range of people. Dorothy Day didn't start every Catholic Worker House of Hospitality. She developed the idea, built one or two models, and then watched as thousands of others gave new expression to the core concept. I thought about the dozens of service organizations I admired, the hundreds of multicultural initiatives that had helped young people find their identities—more examples of core ideas spreading like wildfire, capturing people's imaginations, relying on the creativity of entrepreneurial individuals to take new shape. I started to think in terms of a movement. The best way to represent that intention was a slight change in name, from Interfaith Youth *Corps* to Interfaith Youth *Core*.

Anastasia agreed with that change and added another point: "If the Interfaith Youth Core is going to be a movement, the structure has to be flexible. A movement is a growing group of people making an idea happen in their own way. The trick for the people starting the movement is to articulate the core idea clearly, develop a spread strategy, and then identify and network the best people doing the work."

We came out of that conference with the three pillars that still serve as the heart of the Interfaith Youth Core: intercultural encounter, social action, and interfaith reflection. In other words, the Interfaith Youth Core was about bringing young people from different backgrounds together to engage in social action and reflect on how their different traditions inspired that work. "Now we have to test the concept," Anastasia told me at the close of the conference. "You will learn a lot more about the idea of the Interfaith Youth Core by running projects in the real world than by arguing over language at a conference. And I know the perfect place to start: South Africa."

The Parliament of the World's Religions was being held in Cape Town in December 1999. It was the world's largest interfaith event, with thousands of theologians, activists, and believers of different faiths coming together. The previous Parliament, held in Chicago in 1993, had had a small youth component, but the Parliament organizers were hoping for a higher-impact youth program this time around. They were planning to have more than five hundred young people from around the world attend. The Interfaith Youth Core offered to help them design and run the youth program.

I arrived in Cape Town in late October 1999, nervous and excited. This was my first experience at organizing something outside the United States. I found a nation bursting with energy. It had been less than a decade since the fall of apartheid and barely five years since the African National Congress (ANC), the first black majority government, had taken power. The nation was creating itself anew.

Apartheid in South Africa was a violation of the spiritual principle of human togetherness. South Africans had a term for this principle, *ubuntu*, which translates roughly as "people are people through other people." It was because of ubuntu that South Africans had voted for the pluralist politics of Nelson Mandela's ANC instead of the separatist "throw the whites into the sea" politics of the more radical parties. It was because of ubuntu that Archbishop Desmond Tutu had agreed to lead the Truth and Reconciliation Commission, which sought healing, not punishment, for the sins of apartheid. It was because of ubuntu that Mandela invited his jailers from Robben Island to stand next to him when he was inaugurated as president.

Ubuntu applied not only to racial and tribal harmony but also to religious pluralism. South Africa had significant Hindu, Muslim, Christian, and African Traditionalist populations, as well as a small Jewish population. Religion had a mixed history in South Africa. Apartheid was, after all, not simply a political program but also a theology. Its architects had PhDs from seminaries in Europe and had constructed apartheid from a warped reading of the Bible. But instead of rejecting religion because of its association with apartheid, South Africans had found a way of reinterpreting it as a holy path of liberation and equality. As Desmond Tutu famously said, when the white people came to South Africa, the black people had the land, and they had the Bible. The white people told us to close our eyes and pray. When we opened our eyes, we had the Bible and they had the land. And now we are going to take this book seriously.

South African leaders viewed the Parliament as a spark to increase the participation of the country's diverse religious communities in the nation's renewal. Imam Rashied Omar called it "an African opportunity."

I slept three hours a night during the month leading up to the Parliament, and not even that the week of the event. Registrations were coming in from young people in Japan, Brazil, India, Kenya, Iran— we could barely keep up. These young people had all kinds of suggestions for the youth program. Some wanted to do a project in the poor communities of Cape Town, called the townships. Others had heard that the Parliament was being held in District Six, where years ago the apartheid government had forcefully removed an entire neighborhood of people of color and claimed the land for white people. They wanted to do some kind of a service project and ceremony on that land commemorating its history.

The common theme of the messages we received was that the young people wanted to do something, not just sit back and receive. They wanted to engage South Africa directly, establish real relationships, leave the country a little better for their having been there. We organized a trip to a community center in Mannenberg, a township in the poor Cape Flats area, so that young community organizers coming to the Parliament could connect with their peers in South Africa. We put together a cleanup of the vacant lots in District Six, then asked young people from different faiths to speak about the importance of stewarding creation from their religious traditions. Kevin, who had come from Chicago as part of the Interfaith Youth Core team, met a group of South African hip-hop artists and engaged them in drafting a piece for the youth plenary presentation. "Our generation has to tell the story of interdependence," he said to me. A group of twenty-five young people were invited to make a presentation to the Assembly of Religious and Spiritual Leaders who had gathered at the Parliament and included the Dalai Lama. Instead of standing up at the microphone and voicing platitudes about peace, we encircled the room and made commitments of concrete action: working for the rights of the poor in Britain, building a network of young religious leaders in India, moving forward with a program that destroyed guns in Brazil.

The Interfaith Youth Core approach caught the attention of several people at the Parliament. A senior member of Sarvodaya Shramadana, a Sri Lankan–based movement meaning "the awakening of all through the sharing of labor," invited me to make a presentation at one of its interfaith youth camps. I had admired Sarvodaya Shramadana and its Buddhist leader, A. T. Ariyaratne, for many years. The Interfaith Youth Core was partially based on its methodology of bring-

ing people from different backgrounds together in a community development project, then encouraging them to use that initial space of
gathering to form more sustainable networks that could engage with
the root problems they were collectively facing. In this way, a project
to clean up a river could lead to a group of farmers creating a regional
organization that bargained for lower seed prices from suppliers. The
Sarvodaya Shramadana member wanted his youth camp to know that
young people all over world were coming together to do service projects, talk across religious traditions, and build organizations.

A representative from Habitat for Humanity in India invited the
Interfaith Youth Core to partner with it in a project the group was doing in Hyderabad. Historically a Christian organization based in the
American South, Habitat was now a truly international entity and
was thinking more seriously about how to deal with the diverse religious communities it was encountering in places such as South Asia
and the Middle East. Rima, the Habitat representative, wanted the
Interfaith Youth Core to run interfaith reflection sessions with a group
of religiously diverse young people who would be building homes in
the slums of Hyderabad in January 2001.

Anastasia had been right. When the Interfaith Youth Core presented itself as a mobile idea that could be applied in many places,
other people jumped at the opportunity to have us involved in their
work. Forgetting about my doctorate for a moment, I put both trips on
my calendar and thanked my lucky stars for the opportunity to travel
the world and do interfaith service projects.

Anastasia invited me to spend New Year's with her family at the
Wilgespruit Fellowship Centre, a Christian community and retreat
center located outside Johannesburg. Like the Catholic Worker,
Wilgespruit tried to provide a model for the "Kingdom on Earth," a
place where people could be better. Anastasia's father, Dale White,
was an Anglican priest who believed, in the spirit of Christianity and
South Africa, that humanity was meant to be diverse and in relationship. During the height of the apartheid era, Dale (who is white)
met with Steven Biko to nurture the black consciousness movement,

because he felt it was crucial to rebuild the historical memory and pride of black South Africans. As apartheid was ending and violence between South Africa's various tribes began brewing, Wilgespruit started to train peace mediators. Now, as South Africa was moving into the twenty-first century, Dale was intent on Wilgespruit becoming an interfaith community. To him, South African renewal was not simply about government housing and equal employment laws. It was a spiritual goal that required the unique wisdom of diverse religious communities working together.

It was Ramadan, and I started to settle into fasting. Anastasia fasted with me. We made it a spiritual retreat, sleeping in the small chapel at Wilgespruit, waking up at dawn to say our respective prayers, and then joining with Dale to pray together. "God bless Africa, its children, and its leaders," Dale would say, his voice still slightly weak from the stroke he had suffered recently. "God bless humanity, its various races and religions." I could not help but think that in this country ten years earlier, it would have been illegal for me to stand in the same room as these people because of the color of my skin. And had it not been for the people in this room, and for so many other people in so many rooms like this, it might still be illegal for us to stand here together.

I observed Laylatul Qadr, the night in Ramadan when the Qur'an was first revealed, on New Year's Eve, the turn of the millennium. That night, in prayer, I had a moment of stark clarity: I was part of the story of Islam. I was part of the story of pluralism. I was part of the story of ubuntu.

Every time I announced to my thesis adviser, Geoffrey, that I was leaving for a month or two to run an interfaith youth project somewhere in the world, he would mutter that being a doctoral student was meant to be a full-time occupation and then tell me to have a safe trip and return ready to write. He understood that much of my mental energy was going toward building the Interfaith Youth Core. He also understood that I felt like a stranger in Oxford.

Oxford, someone once told me, is a city of ten thousand students, all studying alone in their rooms. One day you wake up and realize you are among them. The university is organized around its residential colleges, self-contained little worlds dominated by the adventures, idiosyncrasies, and hormones of British undergraduates. Between November and March, the parks close in the late afternoon, and the sun seems permanently hidden behind a thick sheet of immobile clouds. Most of the people I knew preferred the shelter of their rooms to the constant drizzle of Oxford. But I went crazy if I was cooped up for more than a couple of hours a day. That meant, mostly, I flew solo. After a morning of reading and writing at home, I would make my way to Ricardo's sandwich store in the covered market, then hole up at the Grand Café on High Street, drinking French press coffee and catching up on American politics in the *International Herald Tribune*. Evenings, I would go to a play at the Oxford Playhouse or one of the smaller theaters in town, or to an art film at the Phoenix cinema. Occasionally, I would meet with a group of Rhodes scholars for dinner at the Wig and Pen pub or a late-night ice cream at G & D's, but it was not uncommon for me to go days without talking to a friend. It was a stark change from living at Stone Soup, where I was surrounded by eighteen other hippie activists and artists, each constantly insisting that I had to read his new poem or hear her new folk song.

And then I met Nivita. She was Indian, had grown up in Botswana, had attended Amherst College, and had won a Rhodes scholarship from the Southern Africa region. At Oxford, she was studying development with a focus on reducing the devastation of AIDS in Africa. She was quiet and dark and beautiful. She made me feel immediately shy.

After a day of research in London, I would walk back from the Gloucester Green bus station and take the long way past Nivita's dorm room at St. Antony's College. If the light was on, I would call her name until she came to the window, and we would talk for a few minutes before I continued on home, the night suddenly feeling warmer. Once, when I returned especially late and the light was out,

I threw small stones at her window until she lifted it and stared out groggily. "I just wanted to see you before I went to sleep," I said. She smiled, and the edge suddenly left the Oxford chill.

For our first date, I took Nivita to Chez Gaston, a bright French café with funky yellow walls and fresh food on the north side of Oxford. She ordered the spinach crepe, and I ordered the chicken. I noticed Nivita fidgeting in her chair a little, but I kept plowing through the story I was telling and the chicken I was eating. Halfway through, I remembered my manners and asked if she wanted to try some. She couldn't mask her disgust. "I don't eat meat," she said sharply.

"Oops," I said, suddenly feeling stupid. Of course, Nivita was a Hindu, a Brahmin no less. She had never eaten meat; it had never entered the house she had grown up in. Even eating in a restaurant that served meat was a possible compromise, because the meat could have touched the food that Nivita ordered. Kevin, Sarah, and several other people I knew were vegetarians, but they had no moral qualms about what I ate. Nivita was much more sensitive about the matter. Sometimes when we sat down to dinner, she would give me a look, half-accusing and half-forlorn, and say, "You ate chicken for lunch, didn't you?"

"How did you know?" I would protest. It was just a bite. I had brushed my teeth afterward. She would shake her head and hand me a piece of lime to squeeze in my vegetable curry.

What you ate, for Nivita, was a question of faith, and faith was primarily about deepening your spirituality. She and her family had been among the earliest devotees of Sri Sri Ravi Shankar, an Indian guru who had memorized the Bhagavad Gita by the time he was four and invented a breathing technique that his followers swore imbued their lives with a powerful spiritual energy. Nivita performed the twenty-minute ritual early every morning.

I found myself admiring Nivita's spiritual discipline. She poured her heart into prayer. I started trying not to rush through mine, doing my best to pronounce each Arabic term of the Du'a fully before moving on to the next one. When she sang Hindu devotional songs, she swayed back and forth, eyes closed, totally absorbed in their beauty. I stopped treating the *ghazals* of the Pakistani Sufi singer Nusrat Fateh Ali Khan as background music. Now I listened to them with full concentration, with my prayer beads in hand, hearing the music for what it really was: worship.

Nivita and I would take turns praying before dinner. "Your turn," I would say, and we would bow our heads and close our eyes, and I could hear the soothing chanting of Sanskrit lift into the air. We would open our eyes, squeeze hands, and begin eating.

And when it was my turn to pray, I would say Sura al-Fatiha. Once, after I said "Amin" and opened my eyes, I noticed that Nivita's were still closed and that she was whispering something. I realized it was Sanskrit.

At first I wanted to say, "Hey, what's the deal? My prayer doesn't count for you?" But I bit my tongue. Nivita didn't mean to offend me. She was not suggesting that Muslim prayer fell short of heaven. She was not making an objective claim about the worth of one religion over another. She was only indicating that her preference was to connect to God in *her* holy language.

I remembered my time at the Catholic Worker, how I had felt uplifted by the prayer life but also slightly apart from it. I thought about "Ya Ali, Ya Muhammad" coming into my Buddhist meditation and how praying in Arabic felt like the completion of a long journey home.

I realized that I loved Sanskrit prayer, that I considered it beautiful, even holy. But it wasn't *my* holy language, not my way of connecting with God. And I understood somewhere in my soul that, ultimately, I needed to be with someone who shared the same language of prayer.

The discussions in our book group turned toward life after Oxford. Half of the people were going to law school, most at Yale, some at Georgetown or the University of Virginia. Others had taken jobs as consultants and investment bankers. The word "career" was frequently invoked. Everybody seemed to have a plan. I had a mostly complete doctorate and a string of experience running interfaith youth projects in India, Sri Lanka, and South Africa. "Well, it was fun while it lasted," I said to myself.

I went to see Azim Nanji at the Institute of Ismaili Studies. I was wondering if he had any suggestions for tenure-track jobs I should apply for and whether he would be willing to write me a letter of reference. It was Azim's job to develop young Ismaili scholars. The only time I had ever detected pride in his voice was when he told me about Ismailis who had gotten jobs at major universities in North America and Europe, and he mused about the impact they would have when their work started to be published. I thought perhaps he would be excited about my new career focus. But he knew me too well.

"What about the Interfaith Youth Core?" he asked.

"I don't know if starting an interfaith youth movement is a career," I told him. "I've put all this work into doing this doctorate, and I think maybe I should just do what people who get doctorates do—get a job at a university."

"Listen," Azim said, "there are a lot of people in the world with good careers. But you have a big idea about one of the most important issues of our time. You've spent the past three years building that idea. That's more than a career. That's a calling. And when you have a calling, you have to follow it."

7

The Youth Programs of Religious Totalitarians (or Tribal Religion, Transcendent Religion)

> He drew a circle that shut me out—
> Heretic, rebel, a thing to flout,
> But love and I had the wit to win:
> We drew a circle that took him in!
> EDWIN MARKHAM

The first person I called on September 11, 2001, was my friend Roy. "Everyone we know is okay, and everyone they know is okay," he said, his voice a mixture of fury and fear, relief and resolve. Roy was a member of my Rhodes scholar class at Oxford and somehow always managed to be the life of the party and the smartest guy in the room at the same time. He was just the kind of person I could see making a deal over breakfast at Windows on the World, the restaurant atop the World Trade Center. Roy was a devoted Jew whose best friends at Oxford were a Muslim and a Hindu. He believed that pluralism was at the heart of America's greatness, and nowhere was it on more brilliant display than in the masala of cultures that is New York City. As an undergraduate at Harvard, Roy had been the head of the Phillips Brooks House Association, Harvard's student-run community service organization. He was a big believer in the power of service to bring people together, and we had spent many hours talking about strategy for the Interfaith Youth Core. "You realize that what you're doing is more important than ever," he told me on the phone. I heard sirens behind him.

When the pictures of the nineteen hijackers were published, I saw a deeper layer to Roy's comment. I remember staring for a long time at the photographs of the terrorists, searching their faces for signs of dementia or marks of evil. But for the most part, they looked unsettlingly normal, perhaps even a little naive, more like the faces in a high school yearbook than on a Wanted poster. I was surprised that only a couple had facial hair. Wouldn't they want to be pictured with regulation-size beards so that at least they could look the part of jihadis? After all, their mentors Mohammed Haydar Zammar and Khaled Sheikh Mohammed each had a bush of menacing-looking facial hair. And then it occurred to me: the reason the pictures resembled those in a high school yearbook was that some of these murderers were barely out of their teens. Maybe some did not have full beards because they could not grow them.

I remembered Yigal Amir, the extremist Jew who assassinated Israeli prime minister Yitzhak Rabin in 1995. I thought back to 1997, when a member of the Christian Identity movement named Benjamin Smith went on a shooting rampage across the Midwest, targeting Jews, Asians, and African Americans. Twenty-six and twenty-one years old, respectively. I thought about the news reports I heard consistently about religious violence in India, Sri Lanka, the Middle East, Northern Ireland, West Africa, wherever. The ages of the people doing most of the fighting, killing, and dying were generally between fifteen and thirty. The world had recently woken up to the increasing link between religion and violence. But there was something else going on that most people seemed to be missing: the shock troops of religious extremism were young people.

I was starting the Interfaith Youth Core because I thought young people could be a major force in building religious cooperation, and I was having a hard time getting anybody to pay attention. Even people within the small interfaith movement generally treated young people's involvement as a sideshow. But religious extremists didn't view young people as an afterthought. Religious extremists saw a fire in young people that others were missing. They were stoking that fire and turning it into targeted assassinations and mass murder. In my mind, I was picturing a movement of young people working for religious understanding through cooperative service. In my newspapers, I kept reading about teenagers and twentysomethings killing other people in the name of God. Their movement was strong and growing. I began to investigate why.

Osama bin Laden started his terrorist career as a teenager at Al Thagher Model School in Saudi Arabia, where wealthy Saudis send their children for a Western-style education. Young Saudi princes and the sons of the business elite dress in gray slacks and charcoal blazers and assemble every morning for a military-style call to order, then gather again to perform the ritual ablutions before the noon prayer. The teachers at Al Thagher include both Westerners and Arabs, some of whom have been exiled from Jordan, Egypt, and Syria for their involvement in political activities, particularly with the Muslim Brotherhood.

Founded in Egypt in 1928 by a twenty-two-year-old named Hassan al-Banna under the slogan "Islam is the solution," the Muslim Brotherhood has been called the precursor of contemporary radical Islam. Some have argued that its original intention was to be a religious revival movement that provided social services and community for the rapidly changing society of postcolonial Egypt. But Egypt's secular nationalist ruler Gamal Abdel Nasser, who took power in 1952, radicalized its leadership through his brutal crackdowns. The most influential of those leaders was Sayyid Qutb, whom Nasser imprisoned and ultimately executed. Qutb developed the idea that true Muslims are required to wage war against impious regimes and replace them with "authentic" Muslim leadership. This notion became the rallying cry of radical Muslims and remains one of the guiding lights of Muslim totalitarians today.

King Faisal of Saudi Arabia knew that many of the Arab exiles in his country were influenced by the Muslim Brotherhood. He let them in because he felt they had been unfairly persecuted, but he was no more tolerant of open political activity than other Arab leaders. Those who remained committed to the totalitarian vision of the Muslim Brotherhood had to organize clandestinely. They had to find ripe targets for the message of radical Islam. They were looking for people with time on their hands, a desire to make an impact, and the ability to grow the movement. The perfect targets: young people. The perfect venues: schools.

Osama bin Laden's fellow students describe the young Osama as honest and honorable. He did not cheat; he did not steal from other students; he kept to himself. He was about fourteen when a physical education teacher at Al Thagher, a tall Syrian in his late twenties, started an afterschool Islamic study group. He procured the keys to the sports equipment and promised the students an opportunity to play soccer if they joined his club. The teacher was athletic and charismatic, an Arab and a Muslim like most of the students. They admired him and wanted to be around him. They joined his club in droves.

At first he had the students memorize passages of the Qur'an, then some of the stories of the Prophet's life. Gradually, the teacher began telling other stories. "It was mesmerizing," a student in the club confessed to *The New Yorker*'s Steve Coll. He described one story that the teacher told in detail. It was about a young Muslim boy who wanted to please God but found his father standing in the way. The boy located his father's gun—and here the teacher went into excruciating detail about the preparations made by the boy, from developing the plot to loading the gun—and killed the old man.

"I watched the other boys," Osama's former classmate recounted, "fourteen-year-old boys, their mouths open." He found a way to get out. But others, including Osama, only became more devoted to the sessions. They grew mullah-length beards and began telling their schoolmates that true Muslims were required to restore Islamic law across the Middle East by any means necessary.

At university, Osama fell under the spell of another radical, charismatic teacher, Abdullah Azzam. A Palestinian who had joined the Muslim Brotherhood as a young man and later helped found Hamas, Azzam wanted to find a way to make Sayyid Qutb's vision of the violent overthrow of corrupt regimes a reality. "Jihad and the rifle alone," he wrote. "No negotiations, no conferences, and no dialogues." He saw the 1979 Soviet invasion of Afghanistan as his opportunity to bring the warrior ethic back to Islam.

Azzam traveled around the world to spread his message, raising money and recruiting young people to join the armed effort. He opened dozens of recruitment centers, known as services offices. If Sayyid Qutb's innovation was that true Muslims must overthrow unjust regimes, Azzam's breakthrough was building an international network that focused on a concrete cause, Afghanistan. He was the founder of the global jihad.

Osama bin Laden was one of the first to answer Azzam's call. At the age of twenty-three, he was financing Azzam's Peshawar Services Office. Peshawar, located in Pakistan near the Afghan border, was Grand Central Station for young Muslims looking for action in Afghanistan. It was here that bin Laden met a bookish young doctor from a prominent Cairo family, Ayman al-Zawahiri. The two were both struck by the range, quantity, and commitment of Muslim youths pouring into Peshawar, eager to wage jihad. Like entrepreneurs, they realized the potential of this massive market of young Muslims for the product of totalitarian Islam. Zawahiri wrote:

The Muslim youths in Afghanistan waged the war to liberate Muslim land under purely Islamic slogans ... It also gave young

Muslim mujahidin—Arabs, Pakistanis, Turks and Muslims from Central and East Asia—a great opportunity to get acquainted with each other on the land of Afghan jihad through their comrade-ship-at-arms against the enemies of Islam.

Most of these young people never saw action. Afghan command-ers were justifiably wary of mixing foreign youths, some the spoiled children of wealthy donors to the jihad, in with seasoned Afghan warriors. The result was an international network of Muslim youths schooled in the ideology of totalitarian Islam, taught to hate the im-perialist infidel, and trained to kill without being given the opportu-nity to do so. And that is who became Al Qaeda.

Osama bin Laden is, as Bruce Lawrence notes in his introduction to *Messages to the World: The Statements of Osama bin Laden*, many things to many people: public enemy number one in the West, anti-imperialist hero to some in the Muslim world, polemicist extra-ordinaire. But there is an oft-overlooked dimension to bin Laden's personality, a talent that is absolutely central to his macabre success: he is a brilliant youth organizer. He undoubtedly remembers the heat he felt when he first heard the story that the organizer of the Islamic club at Al Thagher told about a young person so pure that he was willing to do anything to please God, even kill his father. When bin Laden had his chance, he took it. He went to Peshawar and put his money, and later his life, on the line so that the infidel Soviets would be expelled from what God meant to be Muslim land. And he was not the only one. Many youths arrived, so young they could barely grow a regulation-length beard, ready to die so that Islam might live. Imag-ine what they could do if they were organized.

A statement that bin Laden released to the Arab news organiza-tion Al Jazeera in December 2001 provides a textbook example of how a skilled totalitarian engages young people in religious violence. In it, he tells the story of a boy who discovers that an animal is blocking a monk's path. (It takes only a basic literary imagination to view the an-imal as America and the monk as the Muslim world.) The boy kills the animal with a rock. "My son, today you are better than me," the monk says to him. Bin Laden follows this story up with the following commentary:

> God Almighty lit up this boy's heart with the light of faith, and he began to make sacrifices for the sake of "There is no god but God." This is a unique and valuable story which the youth of Islam are waiting for their scholars to tell them, which would show the youth that these [the 9/11 attackers] are the people who have given up everything for the sake of "There is no god but God."

Then bin Laden tells a story of how the Prophet's uncle Hamza bin Abd al-Muttalib, who also served as the first military commander of the Muslim community, killed an unjust imam. In this way, he cites a historical figure that Muslims consider a hero and claims that this man's heroism came from his violence. "He won a great victory ... God Almighty raised him up to the status of lord of the martyrs," bin Laden says of al-Muttalib.

Next bin Laden extols the virtues of the 9/11 hijackers:

> God opened the way for these young men ... these heroes, these true men, these great giants who erased the shame from the forehead of our *umma* ... to tell America, the head of global unbelief, and its allies, that they are living in falsehood. They sacrificed themselves for "There is no god but God."

And finally he makes the call: "The youth should strive to find the weak points of the American economy and strike the enemy there."

Just as a skilled totalitarian youth organizer convinced a young Osama to answer the call of jihad through stories of the power of youths to return the ummah to glory, so bin Laden is doing the same for this generation. But Muslims are not the only ones lured into religious extremism by charismatic youth organizers.

"There (is) nothing holier than a terrorist underground." So writes Yossi Klein Halevi in *Memoirs of a Jewish Extremist,* a textbook example of how a young person becomes involved with religious extremism.

Reared in New York during the 1960s on his father's stories of surviving the Holocaust by living in a hole, Halevi became convinced that the world was maniacally arrayed against the Jews. The motto "Esau the Goy hates Jacob the Jew" was the central organizing principle of his life. And everywhere he turned, there was a Jewish organization dedicated to helping him transform that idea into extremist action.

There was Betar, the youth movement of Revisionist Zionism. Yossi was first drawn in by the uniforms that its young initiates wore—blue with a yellow patch on the upper sleeve depicting a map of Israel that included all of Jordan. He started attending Sunday meetings at the organization's basement headquarters, gathering with two dozen other preteen Jews to listen to lectures on the imperative to learn war. He absorbed Revisionist Zionism's alternative version of the Holocaust, which blamed mainstream Jewish leaders for essentially paving the path to Auschwitz because of their refusal to become militant. He became convinced that Jewish survival depended on his generation becoming soldiers.

Betar summer camp indoctrinated him further. The youths sang songs about going to war and killing Arabs. They heard stories of young Jewish martyrs such as Eliyahu Bet-Zuri and Eliyahu Hakim, who had gone calmly to their hanging for assassinating Lord Moyne, the British colonial minister for the Middle East, in 1944.

A tough junior counselor named Danny took young Yossi under his wing, handing him a gun and shouting "Mazel tov" (Congratulations) when the bullet he fired hit the target. The lesson in hand-to-hand combat came after Yossi confessed he had never punched anyone in the face. Danny took off his glasses and said, "Hit me." For Yossi, it was another example of the sacrifice that Betaris would make in training one of their own to become a warrior.

One of his happiest childhood moments was being initiated into Betar. He donned the blue uniform with the yellow patch; stood at attention during a ritual where the American, Israeli, and Betar flags were lowered; and sang the Betar anthem: "From the pit of decay and dust, / With blood and sweat, / A race will arise / Proud, generous and fierce."

In addition to the Betar movement, Yossi imbibed a steady diet of extremist Jewish literature. In school he was assigned the children's magazine *Olomeinu* (Our World), where he read the story of a young Jew who is kidnapped by a Christian nurse and forced to become a priest. One night the boy hears Hebrew songs coming from a synagogue, enters to find his parents sitting inside, and returns to his true self.

Yossi's family received the *Jewish Press* at home, which turned every sideways glance at a Jew into a cry of potential genocide and a call for Jews to become militant. According to the *Jewish Press*, Germans were systematically destroying Jewish memory by vandalizing the community's cemeteries, Hitler had been reincarnated in America in the guise of George Lincoln Rockwell, leader of the American Nazi Party, and a holocaust was already under way in American cities, characterized not by gas chambers but by friendships between Jews and non-Jews. The stories became Yossi's lens on the world. He imagined swastikas etched everywhere and became obsessed with Rockwell's travel schedule. He dreamed of infiltrating the American Nazi Party, destroying it from the inside, and warning his people of the constant need to be vigilant and armed. He swallowed aspirin without water, practicing for the time he would need to do the same with cyanide.

It was the late 1960s, and everywhere Yossi turned young people fed up with the world were taking matters into their own hands. In the Bay Area, Bobby Seale and Huey Newton started the Black Panther Party, promising funerals for police officers who harassed African Americans. Radical white youths had the Weather Underground, who set off bombs to protest America's involvement in Vietnam. Who was protecting Jews who were being beat up in Brooklyn and the

Bronx? Yossi wondered. Why was the oppression of Jews in the Soviet Union consigned to the back pages?

When a dozen Jews were arrested in Russia in June 1970, mainstream Jewish organizations were anemic in their response and contemptuous toward youth involvement. "We gave two thousand dollars last year to the American Jewish Conference on Soviet Jewry," the foreign affairs expert at the Anti-Defamation League told Yossi and a group of his activist friends.

"Out of your budget of how many millions?" one of them retorted.

"You kids don't know what you want," was the dismissive answer.

"We don't take direction from you," said the president of Hadassah, another mainstream Jewish organization. "Youth have no right to come here."

The one organization that cared about the fate of Soviet Jewry and involved young people, the Student Struggle for Soviet Jewry (SSSJ), seemed increasingly lost and powerless. The vigil the group held to raise awareness about the recent arrests drew fewer than fifty people and almost no media.

Only Meir Kahane's Jewish Defense League (JDL) understood the frustrated passions of young American Jews, nurtured on the horrors of the Holocaust and the heroes of Israel's founding, longing to carve out a place in Jewish history. Raised in Brooklyn, trained by Betar, delusional and messianic, Kahane was a brilliant organizer of young people. He knew that the energy building within young American Jews was on the brink of explosion. The arrests in the Soviet Union provided a convenient vehicle for Kahane to communicate his larger worldview—that Jewish survival depended on dominating others with force. Jews had suffered enormously because previous generations had ignored the message. At rallies, Kahane taunted mainstream Jewish leaders for being "nice Irvings" who allowed the Holocaust to happen because they were more interested in respectability than militancy. Yossi Halevi and his generation vowed never to make that mistake. Kahane became their pied piper. They loved his carefully cultivated image of self-sacrificial militant commitment to the cause of Jewish survival, his call for "a thousand young Jews ready to go over the barricade," and his willingness to be at the front of the line.

While other Jewish organizations did little in response to the arrest of Soviet Jews, the JDL organized dramatic actions. Kahane and twenty others entered the Soviet trade office in Manhattan and threatened the staff with lead pipes. They disrupted concerts by Russian performers in New York, chained themselves to the wheels of a Soviet airliner at JFK airport, and destroyed property at the Soviet UN mission. JDL rallies attracted hundreds of young Jews, raising their fists and repeating after Kahane, "Two Russians for every Jew."

When a pipe bomb exploded outside the New York office of the Soviet airline Aeroflot, presumably planted by JDL associates, Yossi felt a surge of pride. "I was thrilled," he wrote. "Nobody could dismiss us now. We were just like the anti-Vietnam movement: *serious*." His friends were mostly other young people involved in the JDL, several of them on a first-name basis with Kahane and increasingly responsible for the organization's acts of violence. When they heard of an attack on Jews, they drove to the victims' home and stood there in military fashion. Moish, one of Yossi's school friends, played the role of sniper, setting up across the street from the house with a shotgun.

Yossi craved what the JDL offered: "Kahane was telling us, young American Jews, that our comfortable lives were an aberration, a meaningless interlude between times of persecution, and that by confronting New York cops and risking beating and arrest we could reenter Jewish history and experience its menacing intensity."

Like Hasib Hussain, the July 7, 2005, London Tube bomber who had become obsessed with Muslim oppression in Britain and abroad, Yossi's fears were partially true. The Holocaust *was* gut-wrenchingly horrible; anti-Semitism *is* a persistent strain across human history; Jewish kids *were* chased and beaten in New York's boroughs in the 1960s and 1970s. Both had immigrant parents who lived in ethnic-religious cocoons, expressing a peculiar combination of disgust and gratitude toward their adopted homeland, unable to provide their kids with a religious identity relevant to their time and place. Hasib Hus-

sain felt guilty that he had not experienced suffering like the Palestinians or Bosnians, that he had not been part of the mujahideen
battling the Soviets in the 1980s. Yossi felt guilty that he had not suffered through the Holocaust or battled Arab armies to help secure
the state of Israel in 1948. They both craved a place in the historical
drama of their tribes. They both felt that mainstream religious institutions ignored their passion. They were both unremarkable, middle-
class kids with no particular pathology outside of a teenager's inherent
sense of urgency. In both cases, religious extremists skillfully chan-
neled their teenage intensity into a totalitarian identity and violent
action.

If suicide bombing had been a standard tactic of religious extremism in the early 1970s, Yossi and his friends might have lined up to accept Kahane's blessing and a belt loaded with bombs.

Who does not understand violence? Who has not experienced suffering and wanted to inflict it twice over in return? Who has not felt
the heat and thunder of anger rise up in him or her? Who has not
known the total release of fury bursting forth?

I still remember the time I got burned on a fly pattern during a
pickup football game in junior high. David caught the ball, Jerry Rice
style, over his left shoulder, did a dance in the end zone, said a few
choice words to me, and trotted across the field. Five minutes went
by. Ten minutes. The sting remained. David was about ten feet away.
He had his back turned, talking and laughing with his teammate.
Were they mocking me? I felt the rage rush up, and it was almost as if
I couldn't help myself. I got a running start, aimed my shoulder into
the small of his back, and rammed into him with all the force I could
muster. His body crumpled under the weight of mine, and I felt a sense
of total resolution.

A few years later, when I saw the movie *Lawrence of Arabia*, I had
a deep understanding of the scene where Lawrence describes the first
time he killed a man. The problem, he says, was not just the act. It was
that he liked it.

We humans know violence well. It is a part of each of us. It is precisely the reason I was drawn to religion in the first place. Somehow, the religious people I admired overcame the human desire to hurt others. Tibetan Buddhist masters talked about their struggle to love their Chinese tormentors. Mahatma Gandhi spent his time in a South African prison making sandals for his jailer. Pope John Paul II met with the man who tried to assassinate him, and forgave him.

Dorothy Day once said that she created the Catholic Worker because she wanted a place where people could be better. It was one of the key reasons I spent so much time there as a college student. I wanted to overcome those parts of me that would tackle somebody from behind. I wanted to be good.

It was in Islam that I found the clearest articulation of this inner struggle. The story goes like this: As a victorious Muslim army was celebrating its triumph in battle, the Prophet Muhammad told the men they had won only the "lesser jihad." Now, he said, they had to move on to the "greater jihad"—the *jihad al-nafs*, the struggle against their lower selves. The first time I read that, I felt as if the Prophet was speaking directly to me, as if he could see the thousands of times in my life that my lower self had won, as if he was personally returning Islam to my consciousness.

There is another event in the history of Islam that, for me, defines the religious spirit in the world, and the meaning of lasting victory. It is the signing of the Treaty of Hudaybiyah and the Prophet's peaceful return to Mecca. After years of defending himself and his fellow Muslims in Medina against aggressive military assaults by the Quraysh, a powerful tribe based in Mecca, Muhammad decided to launch a religious peace offensive. In the year 628, he announced to the Muslim community in Medina that he was going to make a holy pilgrimage to the Ka'aba, the black shrine in Mecca that Abraham built to God. Against the advice of his closest companions, who were convinced that the Quraysh would take this chance to murder him, Muhammad refused to carry arms. He set forth dressed in the simple, white, two-piece outfit still worn by Muslims making the hajj today, uttering the

cry "Labbayk Allahuma Labbayk" (Here I am, O God, at Your service). A thousand Muslims accompanied him, many questioning the
wisdom of making a religious pilgrimage in the direction of an enemy
that wanted war.

The Quraysh sent a war party of two hundred cavalry to prevent
Muhammad from entering the city. The Prophet steered his companions toward Hudaybiyah, at the edge of the Sanctuary, where all fighting was forbidden, sending a message to the Quraysh that he came
in peace. He reminded his companions that they were on a religious
quest and as such should prepare to repent and ask God's forgiveness for their sins. No doubt some of them were confused about why
Muhammad was making spiritual preparations instead of war preparations. But Muhammad, guided by revelations from God, knew that
ultimate victory for Islam did not mean violently defeating the enemy,
but peacefully reconciling with them. Achieving this required an act
of personal humility and self-effacement that shocked even his closest companions.

After being convinced that Muhammad was not going to engage
them in battle, the Quraysh sent Suhayl, one of their most stridently
anti-Muslim leaders, to negotiate a settlement. The two sat together
for a long time, finally agreeing to terms that the Muslims felt were
deeply unfair but that Muhammad insisted they accept. The Muslims
would be allowed to do the holy pilgrimage in peace, but not now.
They would have to go back to Medina and wait a whole year before
returning. Also, the Muslims would have to repatriate any Meccan
who had converted to Islam and immigrated to Medina to be with the
Prophet without the permission of his guardian. One source writes
that the Prophet's companions "felt depressed almost to the point of
death" when they saw the settlement. Umar, one of the Prophet's closest associates, said, "Why should we agree to what is demeaning to our
religion?" But the greatest shock was still to come.

When it came time to sign the treaty, Suhayl objected to the statement, "This is what Muhammad, the apostle of God, has agreed with
Suhayl ibn Amr." He said that if he recognized Muhammad as the

apostle of God, they would not be in a situation of war to begin with. "Write down your own name and the name of your father," Suhayl instructed the Prophet. To the utter despair of his companions, Muhammad agreed. He told Ali, his son-in-law who would later become the first Shia Imam, to strike the words "apostle of God" from the treaty. Ali could not bring himself to do it. So the illiterate Prophet asked Ali to point to the words on the paper, took the pen, and struck them himself.

On the journey home to Medina, with the bitter taste of humiliation still fresh in the mouths of his companions, the Prophet received a revelation that would come to be known as the Victory Sura, chapter 48 in the Holy Qur'an. In it, God told the Prophet, "Surely We have given thee / a manifest victory." The sura states that God Himself was involved in the situation: "It is He who sent down the sakina / into the hearts of the believers, that / they might add faith to their faith." The Arabic term *sakina* loosely translates as "the peace, tranquillity, and presence of God" and is thought to be related to the Hebrew term *shekinah*. The sura closes with the following lines: "God has promised / those of them who believe in and do deeds / of righteousness, forgiveness and / a mighty wage."

The following year, as promised, Muhammad returned with nearly three thousand pilgrims to perform the pilgrimage. His enemies, holding up their end of the bargain, vacated the city and watched the Muslims do the ritual circumambulations around the Ka'aba and run seven times between the hills of Safa and Marwah. They were shocked to see Bilal, a black Abyssinian who had been a slave in Mecca before being freed by the Muslims, climbing to the top of the Ka'aba several times a day to give the call to prayer, a position of honor in Islam. Muhammad heard that a woman had recently been widowed and offered to marry her, thus taking her into his protection. He invited his Quraysh enemies to the wedding feast. They refused and told him his three days were up. The Muslims left with the same discipline and grace with which they had entered. It was a powerful image that many Quraysh would not soon forget.

When Muhammad returned to Mecca a year later, those who had taken up arms against him converted to Islam in droves. Muhammad granted a near total amnesty to the Quraysh, despite the fact that many had fought battles against him in the past and regardless of whether they converted to Islam or not. To the surprise of some of his companions, he even gave high office to some of the people who, a short time before, had been his sworn enemies. But Muhammad was not interested in punishment. He was interested in a positive future, and he knew that would be accomplished only by widening the space so that people could enter it.

During this time, God sent Muhammad a revelation about relations between different communities in a diverse society:

> O mankind, We have created you
> male and female, and appointed you
> races and tribes, that you may know
> one another. Surely the noblest
> among you in the sight of God is
> the most righteous.

For me, the Treaty of Hudaybiyah and the peaceful return of Muhammad to Mecca are the defining moments of Islam. They exemplify the genius of the Prophet, the generosity of God, and the bright possibility of a common life together. It is an ancient example of how a religiously inspired peace movement can win a victory not by defeating the enemy, but by turning them into friends.

As I think now of the civil rights marchers in Selma and Birmingham, Alabama, I cannot help but hear the message of "Labbayk Allahuma Labbayk" in their songs. I cannot help but see the Prophet at Hudaybiyah as I reflect on Martin Luther King Jr. staring at his bombed-out home in Montgomery, Alabama, and calming the agitated crowd by saying, "We must meet hate with love." I cannot help but glimpse the spirit of the Holy Qur'an's message on pluralism in the lines that King uttered at the end of the Montgomery bus boycott:

"We have before us the glorious opportunity to inject a new dimension of love into the veins of our civilization ... The end is reconciliation, the end is redemption, the end is the creation of the beloved
community." I cannot help but believe that Allah's sakina is a force
that has reappeared across time and place whenever righteous people
are overcoming the tribal urges of humanity's lower self with a message of transcendence.

So what of the relationship between religion and violence? Are there
not people who chant the name of God while they murder others? Is
it not the case that religious texts themselves sometimes call for violence? Undoubtedly, religion is at the center of a vast array of horrible things. But it is clearly not confined only to evil use. Religion, as
Archbishop Desmond Tutu once said, is simply a tool, like a knife.
When a knife is used to cut bread, it is good. When it is used to cut
someone's throat, it is bad.

A favorite explanation of people who are suspicious of religion in
general, or other people's religions in particular, is that religious texts
themselves command violence, and so it should not surprise us when
believers obey. This argument is particularly marshaled against Muslims, with Islamophobes and Muslim totalitarians alike circulating papers that cite only the parts of the Qur'an that deal with violence.

I concede that the bin Ladens of the world are not making everything up. There are indeed explicit statements about violence in the
scriptures of most major religious traditions. But to think that the
statements of a religious text suddenly morph into armed reality is to
have a profound misunderstanding of religion. There are several layers of meaning to any religious text: the explicit, the contextual, and
the symbolic, to name just a few. A religious text comes to life through
its interpreters. Violence committed in the name of a religion is really
violence emanating from the heart of a particular interpreter. As the
scholar Ignaz Goldziher put it, "It could be said about the Qur'an ...
everyone searches for his view in the Holy Book." Or, as the great
Muslim legal scholar Khaled Abou El Fadl writes, "The Qur'anic text

assumes that readers will bring a preexisting, innate moral sense to the text. Hence, the text will morally enrich the reader, but only if the reader will morally enrich the text."

Another common theory is that religious violence is a result of oppression, largely based on the policies of the powerful. There is no doubt that far too many people in the world have their freedom restricted by repressive regimes, live in the grip of wrenching hunger, are constantly fearful of the threat of violence, or experience some combination of the three. My personal opinion is that my own government does far too little to help, often exacerbates the problem, and is sometimes one of the chief reasons it exists. But poverty, repression, and fear, as well as the policies that lead to them, do not by themselves arm people. As Jessica Stern writes in *Terror in the Name of God,* "The same variables (political, religious, social, or all of the above) that seem to have caused one person to become a terrorist might cause another to become a saint." What counts is how a community responds to a situation. Too often, that response is shaped by people aiming for violence and skilled at recruiting young people to commit it.

I believe that religious violence is the product of careful design, manipulated by human hands. It is more about sociology than scripture, more about institutions than inevitability. The theology of the world's bin Ladens is influential because they have built powerful institutions that recruit, inspire, and train people to act in hateful and murderous ways. When people respond to oppression by killing their enemies while whispering the name of God, it is because an organization convinced them that doing so is a sacred duty and then gave them everything they needed to carry it out. And so often, their primary targets are young people. As Stern writes, "Holy wars take off only when there is a large supply of young men who feel humiliated and deprived; when leaders emerge who know how to capitalize on those feelings; and when a segment of society—for whatever reason—is willing to fund them."

But religious extremists do not only speak of humiliation and deprivation. They define the Zeitgeist as reclaiming the historical greatness of a religious tradition and tell their target audience of teenagers that they are the only ones who can achieve it. They juxtapose a people's current suffering against a mythical alternative and tell young people that it is their destiny to transport their people from the former to the latter. That mythical alternative has both historical and theological dimensions, such as the time of the Prophet for Muslims and the Messiah's coming for Jews. And it is the responsibility of young people to realize it, whether that means driving America out of Saudi Arabia or establishing settlements in Hebron. Many mainstream religious institutions ignore young people or, worse, think that their role should be limited to designing the annual T-shirt. By contrast, religious extremists build their institutions around the desire of young people to have a clear identity and make a powerful impact.

Institutions, writes the sociologist Peter Berger, are best understood as programs for human activity. It is a truism that applies to a broad range of sectors. Consider a recent example of how a network of powerful institutions made a set of political ideas dominant. After recovering from the shock of defeat in 2000, Democrats began investigating how Republicans had managed to unseat them after eight years of Clinton-era peace and prosperity. Wasn't it the case, they asked, that millions of people had voted against their own interests when casting their ballots for George W. Bush? How had this happened? The answer, they found, lay in the superior institution building of the Republican Party. Since Barry Goldwater's defeat in the 1964 presidential election, a handful of philanthropic foundations had become very strategic about channeling money to a small number of think tanks, which nurtured a core set of ideas that played well in parts of America that were becoming demographically significant. More recently, the "Republican message machine" (which was really just a network of these institutions) became highly effective at recruiting extremely electable candidates, provided them with lavish campaign funding, and offered professional training sessions where they learned to communicate effectively in media-friendly sound bites. The Democrats were left to bleat about how their ideas were actually more popular with Americans on Sunday morning talk shows, while Republicans replaced them in Congress and in the White House.

In the sphere of religion, the totalitarians have spent decades investing in their institutions and focusing like a laser on young people. Consider the institutions of Hindu extremism, led by an organization known as the National Volunteer Corps, or RSS. The RSS was formed in 1925 with the express goal of marginalizing India's Christian, Muslim, and other minorities in the pursuit of a "pure" Hindu nation. One of the RSS's early leaders, M. S. Golwalkar, openly expressed admiration for Nazi Germany. He wrote, "National pride at its highest has been manifested here. Germany has also shown how well-nigh impossible it is for races and cultures, having differences going to the root, to be assimilated into one united whole, a good lesson for us in Hindustan to learn and profit by."

This ideology is spread through a sophisticated institutional structure. The core unit of the RSS is known as a *shakha* (cell), where *swayamsevaks* (volunteers) gather to be steeped in Hindu totalitarian ideology and engage in activities that spread it. The model was borrowed from Mussolini's Fascist Party in Italy. The cells multiply when seasoned swayamsevaks move to a different area to start a new shakha. A friend of mine doing a graduate degree in Bombay estimated that more than half of her classmates were either actively involved in a shakha or had been raised in the shakha system.

Swayamsevaks also move into positions of influence within the RSS's many different wings. These include a youth wing called the Bajrang Dal, which doubles as a paramilitary group; a political party called the BJP (which held national office from 1998 to 2004); a so-called service wing known as the Sewa Vibhag; and a cultural-political mobilization wing called the VHP. These different segments work together in the most nefarious ways. For example, in the 2002 murder spree that left approximately two thousand Muslims dead in the state of Gujarat, BJP government officials used instruments of the state, including the police force, to encourage the killing; the Bajrang Dal and Sewa Vibhag sent truckloads of young militants into Muslim areas to carry out the murders; and the VHP provided the political and organizational mobilization, its international working president going so far as to call the carnage a "successful experiment" that would be repeated in other parts of India.

Of course, totalitarians have always recognized the importance of building institutions that attract young people. The Nazis are a prime example. After gaining power in 1933, Hitler began to systematically indoctrinate the next generation. He took over schools, firing teachers suspected of being opposed to the regime and forcing the remaining educators to join the National Socialist Teachers League, which monitored teachers throughout Germany and organized camps where teachers were trained in how to most effectively teach Nazi ideology to German students. Families were required to enroll their ten- to eighteen-year-old children in the Hitler Youth, which grew from just over a hundred thousand in 1933 to nearly nine million by 1939, organized around the motto, "Führer, command—we follow!"

Religious totalitarians have put enormous effort into two institutions where young people spend a great deal of time: schools and websites. The Christian Identity movement is particularly adept on the web. Their sites feature electronic coloring books with white supremacist symbols, crossword puzzles with racist clues, and twenty-four-hour webcasts. Interested in reading Eric Rudolph's most recent musings or writing to him in jail? You can find that information, plus several flattering photographs of him, at the Army of God website.

Online Bible studies that masquerade as mainstream endeavors slowly take unsuspecting students deeper and deeper into the theology of white supremacy. The purpose statement at the Kingdom Identity Ministries website reads:

What does the A.I.T. Bible Course do for Christian Education? It brings understanding, it reveals facts. It separates man-made doctrine from the original Holy Scriptures. It creates a sound basis for a person's Christian Faith ... One sure way to a non-denominational Christian Education is via the American Institute of Theology Bible Course.

A few clicks later, and students are reading about how white people are God's chosen race and Asians, Jews, and blacks are worthy only of subjugation, slavery, and destruction.

Schools are a major area of focus for religious totalitarians. In the mid-1990s, about six thousand schools, employing forty thousand teachers and educating more than one million students, were associated with the RSS in India. A National Council of Educational Research and Training report concluded that the curriculum used by many of these schools was "designed to promote bigotry and religious fanaticism in the name of inculcating knowledge of culture in the younger generation." Textbooks contain a map of India that includes Pakistan, Bangladesh, Bhutan, Nepal, Tibet, and parts of Burma. The alphabet is taught using Hindu symbols—A is for Arjuna, B is for the Bhagavad Gita, and so on. Letters that do not correspond to any Hindu symbol do not get taught.

Institutions require money, and religious extremists make the most serious investments. A financial network committed to an aggressive version of Salafi Islam has dramatically changed the Muslim world over the past quarter century. These Salafis insist that the only true Muslims are the ones who follow a purist practice of Islam based on an imagined notion of the early Muslim community. Salafis actively seek to destroy any diversity within the ummah and consider relations between Muslims and other communities anathema. How has this interpretation become dominant? Private foundations and wealthy individuals in the Persian Gulf have funded educational institutions that create textbooks, produce videos, and train Muslim preachers. Muslim communities around the world receive money to build lavish mosques, and Salafi imams are sent to staff them and make sure their educational materials are widely available at low cost. One expert calls this process the single most effective use of philanthropic money in the past two decades: "They [the Salafis] have managed to shift the meaning of Islam in the global marketplace of ideas because there is no meaningful competition of any kind."

Well-run youth programs have a profound impact on the behavior of young people. This is strikingly illustrated in a summer camp experiment organized by social psychologist Muzafer Sherif. Attempting to sow hostility between the boys at the camp, Sherif's researchers divided them into two groups, called the Rattlers and the Eagles, and organized a series of athletic competitions designed to build intragroup solidarity and intergroup antagonism. The researchers intensified this polarization by giving preferential treatment to one group. The Eagles were invited early to a camp party and ate all the choice refreshments before the Rattlers showed up. The Rattlers were furious, name-calling ensued, and soon punches were being thrown.

The researchers then sought to reverse the hostility. The most effective approach they found was putting the kids in situations where they had to work together. They organized a camping trip where the truck broke down. Every boy had to help, either pushing or pulling the vehicle, to get it back to camp. After participating in a series of similar cooperative projects, the hostile feelings dissipated, and the boys reported strong feelings of solidarity.

I recently read an Indian journalist's account of the RSS. I was surprised at the intimacy of the article, the detailed description of life inside the organization. I wondered how he knew so much about it. Toward the end, he confessed that he had been a member during the 1940s, when he was a teenager. It was the twilight of the colonial era, and he wanted to be part of something larger than himself. He joined the RSS because it seemed like the only option for a teenager with a growing political consciousness. He ended the article with a final detail: the more moderate Congress Party did not have an active youth wing in his area.

This same dynamic defines our world today. The totalitarians have put their resources into building youth programs. The pluralists haven't.

I remember a conversation with a well-meaning Protestant in a wealthy suburb just north of Chicago. He approached me after a talk I gave on the importance of youth programs in religious communities and made a sheepish confession: "My wife and I really enjoy the church we go to, but my daughter, she hates it. She thinks the services are boring, and she complains that there's no real youth program. The pastor keeps talking about starting one, but I guess he has other priorities." He kind of shrugged as if to say, "At least we're thinking about it." Then he asked me offhandedly, "What do you suggest we do?"

I didn't hesitate. "Change churches," I said.

He looked a bit taken aback. "Either that or make sure that the church starts a youth program that interests your daughter," I continued. In my mind, it was a question of priorities: was he more interested in his daughter liking church or himself liking it?

Most people choose themselves over their kids. It is an entirely understandable choice, but we should not be blind to the consequences. It means that we will continue to fail our religious youth. I cannot help but think of the number of teenagers I know who say that they are bored in their congregations, that their church or synagogue or mosque or temple has little going on for them. The youth minister they liked was let go because of budget cuts. The Habitat for Humanity trip they were planning got canceled because the adult supervisor couldn't make it at the last minute. The pastor or imam or rabbi can never remember their names.

Too many adults secretly consider the absence of young people in mainstream religious communities the natural course of events, viewing the kids as too self-absorbed, materialistic, and anti-authoritarian to be interested in religion. The result is that adults pay lip service to the importance of involving youths in faith communities but let themselves off the hook when it comes to actually building strong, long-lasting youth programs. Youth activities are typically the top item in a congregation's newsletter but the last line in the budget. Youth programs are the most likely to be funded by short-term grants, and youth ministers are the first to be fired when a religious community has financial problems.

Recent research by sociologist Christian Smith shows how wrong-headed this view is. In his book *Soul Searching,* Smith concludes that many young Americans want religion to play an important role in their lives, but their faith communities do a poor job of involving them. The problem, Smith observes, is that religious communities seriously fail to adequately support youth programs. He writes, "Very many religious congregations and communities of faith in the United States are failing rather badly in religiously engaging and educating their youth."

Were Yigal Amir, Hasib Hussain, and Benjamin Smith meant to be murderers? How about Osama bin Laden? They, too, were born with the breath of God within them. They, too, were made to be servants and representatives of God on earth, to steward His creation with a sense of compassion and mercy. What happened?

Every time we read about a young person who kills in the name of God, we should recognize that an institution painstakingly recruited and trained that young person. And that institution is doing the same for thousands, maybe hundreds of thousands, of others like him. In other words, those religious extremists have invested in their youth programs.

If we had invested in our youth programs, could we have gotten to those young people first?

8
Building the Interfaith Youth Core

How are we, in the United States, to embrace
difference and maintain a common life?
MICHAEL WALZER

I arrived at her doorstep soaking wet. It was pouring rain, and the wind-
shield wipers on my car had suddenly stopped working. I couldn't see
a thing driving south on Lake Shore Drive to her condo in Streeter-
ville. I had to lean out the driver's side window, grab one of the wipers,
and move it up and down with my hand to clear a space on the wind-
shield.

Kevin had been telling me about this woman for years. Her name
was Shehnaz, and she had gone to law school with Kevin's friend
Nikki. Every time Kevin would talk about her, I would shrug it off.
"You're being an idiot," he would say. "She's a civil rights attorney,
she's beautiful, she's Indian, she's a Muslim, she owns her own condo,
and she will probably agree to see you on my recommendation. You,
on the other hand, don't have a job and don't own anything except
some books on anthropology. Don't you think that you should try to
improve your lot in this world and ask her out?" Finally, I took his advice, and here I was, all wet.

152 ACTS OF FAITH

Shehnaz laughed when I explained my car situation. She handed me a towel and motioned for me to sit on the couch across the room. I settled in, looked up, and found myself thinking about poems that praised deep beauty.

We talked about her job as a civil rights lawyer. Her clients were mostly poor minorities with lengthy rap sheets who had been beaten up by Chicago police officers. "Everybody has rights in this country," Shehnaz said flatly. "That's what makes it great. If we let the rights of one group erode, we endanger the very existence of those rights for everybody."

She was working on a new case: a mosque foundation was being harassed by a suburban council, and she was preparing a First Amendment/religious discrimination suit. "When it's your people being discriminated against because of their religion, you realize how important the Constitution is to everybody," she said.

We went for dosas at Mysore Woodlands on Devon Avenue, ate with our hands, laughed about what it was like growing up in the western suburbs of Chicago with Indian Muslim parents. She had gone to high school in Naperville, fifteen minutes from where I grew up. We had probably passed each other at the Ogden Six movie theater. We had graduated high school one year apart and overlapped at the University of Illinois. "You never read my column in the *Daily Illini?*" I asked her over milk shakes at the Zephyr café. "You never came to any Indian Student Association meetings?" she shot back. I decided it was better that she hadn't known me in college.

It was a work night, and I thought maybe I should drop her back home. But I didn't want to leave her. I decided to push my luck. "Kurt Elling sings at the Green Mill tonight," I said. "Wanna go?"

"All right," she said softly.

That was Wednesday. Thursday we ate chow foon at Hong Min in Chinatown and went to see Thomas Mapfumo and the Blacks Unlimited at the HotHouse. Friday we watched the film *Girlfight*. Saturday we ate Thai fish cakes at Rosded in Lincoln Square and caught the band Funkadesi. I ran into some people I knew from college at the show. "Is she with you?" they asked.

"Yes," I said, just loud enough for Shehnaz to hear. She didn't turn around, but I thought I saw her smile.

We walked outside. She saw the moon, slowly took her hand out of mine, ran her palm down her face, and whispered the shahada: "La Ilaha il Allah, Muhammadu Rassoolillah."

The first thing I did when I got back to Oxford was tell my landlord that I needed to break my lease. I called Kevin and said, "I'll be home before New Year's."

"But you just left."

"I met the one," I told him. "I'm coming back to Chicago."

Chicago, a somber city? What was Saul Bellow talking about? I returned to an exuberant city—a blue-collar metropolis getting an artists' makeover; an American city taking its place in the world; a town unafraid to decorate cow statues and call it public art; a city that was one part Indiana and one part Manhattan.

It was a rich time to be back in Chicago. The Cubs, Sox, Bulls, and Bears each got a new coach—two of them black, one Latino. Millennium Park was emerging from the big mud pit on Michigan Avenue, an urban playground that felt both a part of downtown and a world away. In a basement on the South Side, Kanye West was producing beats, practicing rhymes, dreaming of new layers in hip-hop. In another basement not far from there, a Senate campaign was under way, and a local politician named Barack Obama was about to become a national icon.

I loved the thousands of trees and flowers that the mayor had planted. I loved the way the sun played off the lake on a cold winter day. I loved the Russian Jews and Pakistani Muslims who spent their Thursday afternoons on the park benches on Devon Avenue. I loved the women who filled the corridor between O'Hare Airport and the Blue Line back to the city with gospel songs.

I thought about Louis Armstrong stopping to listen to a group of jazz musicians who were playing "Struttin' with Some Barbecue." "Man, you're playing that too slow," he told them.

"How would *you* know?" one asked scornfully.

"I'm Louis Armstrong. That's my chorus you're playing," he said.

The next day he walked by the same corner, and the musicians had hung up a sign: PUPILS OF LOUIS ARMSTRONG.

Jazz got educated in this town. The blues went electric here. And one of the originals, Buddy Guy, still played a show almost every night of the week during the month of January at his club, Legends.

I went back to my old barber, an Iraqi who had been forced to fight in Saddam Hussein's army in the Gulf War and was given asylum in the United States. His son came bounding up as he threw the smock around my shoulders. The boy wanted to show his father some new trick on his Game Boy. "My God," I told Amir, "is that Dexter?" He was three the last time I saw him—shy, still a toddler. Now he had a head of thick, wavy hair and eyes set off by long Arab eyelashes. I asked Dexter about school, about his grandparents; next thing I knew, my hair was done.

"Hey, Eboo," I heard. It was a black girl's voice, soft but not shy. I was munching on a falafel sandwich made by the Palestinian grocer near El Cuarto Año, where I had my first teaching job. "You don't remember me?" she asked, her voice playful. "It's Roxanne. You were my teacher second semester, right here," she said, gesturing toward the school building. "I got my GED. I got a job now, and my son's doing real good—he's in preschool." She smiled.

I woke up one morning and took my *Chicago Tribune* out of its blue wrapper, and there was a story that brought me to tears. Daniel Barenboim, the conductor of the Chicago Symphony Orchestra, an Argentine Israeli maestro, had shown up at a student assembly at a school in the Palestinian territories and played the piano. Simply brought his gift to a group of students who are given too little, communicating that they, too, are worthy of beauty.

Kevin and I got off the Red Line at the Fullerton stop. "Do you remember what I said to you here five years ago?" he asked me. "I told you I was dropping out of college, that I was just going to work on my poetry. I asked you if you thought I could make it as a poet." I remembered. Kevin had just been asked to be part of HBO's *Def Poetry*. He had been making his living as a poet—performing on college campuses, teaching workshops at high schools, organizing poetry slams in community centers for a couple of years now. He was working on a new piece about Chicago, and he wanted to read it to me.

The people who organized the mayor's annual Leadership Prayer Breakfast heard about the Interfaith Youth Core (IFYC) and invited me to give the Muslim prayer at the event. Somehow, I got seated next to the mayor. "Are you Indian?" he asked. "My daughter just spent six months in Kerala." For the next twenty minutes, we talked about India. When the waiter came around to pour him more coffee, Mayor Daley said, "No thanks, Oscar." I stared at him. How did the mayor of Chicago know the name of the guy who pours coffee at the Hilton Towers? He shrugged and said, "He and I went to grade school together."

Home. The place where your barber doesn't have to ask what to do with your hair. Where the music you love came of age. Where the leading citizens fill you with pride. Where your best friend's dreams are coming true. Where your former students recognize you on the street. The piece of earth that your hands have helped shape.

Chicago is accustomed to making big dreams into reality. It was on the near West Side of this city that a young Jane Addams created Hull House, a "cathedral of humanity" for recent immigrants that became both a symbol and a laboratory for the inclusion of newcomers into American democracy. A few decades later, on the South Side of Chicago, a brash young leader named Saul Alinsky applied the methods used by labor unions to neighborhoods, building what became known as "community organizations" where common people worked together to demand their due from entrenched business and political elites. And it was here that the first Parliament of the World's Religions took place, in the year 1893, sparking the interfaith movement in the West. In Chicago's "make no little plans" spirit, one of the Parliament's leaders declared, "From now on, the great religions of the world will no longer declare war on each other, but instead on the giant ills that afflict all humankind."

Jeff Pinzino, my friend from college, was the first person to introduce the IFYC vision to Chicago. He had led the interfaith Habitat for Humanity project with me in Hyderabad, India, in January 2001 and saw firsthand how service built understanding between people from different religious backgrounds. He returned to Chicago determined to establish a foundation for the IFYC. And as with everything else he's done, Jeff went about it full force. He quit his job, left Stone Soup (the artists and activists community we had started together in 1997, where he had been living for nearly four years), and started gathering a network of supporters for the IFYC. Jeff laid the groundwork for two IFYC projects that continue today: the Chicago Youth Council (CYC), made up of students from different religions who gather weekly to do service projects and engage in interfaith reflection, and the Day of Interfaith Youth Service, which brings together hundreds of youths from different religions to do a large-scale service project on one day. He financed the operation mostly with his own credit card.

I spent the first few months of 2002 finishing my dissertation. I passed my oral exams and received my doctorate in June, right about the time that Jeff felt his work with the IFYC was done. He had been offered a job with a foundation that had been impressed by his experience as a community organizer and the entrepreneurial spirit he had shown in building the base of the IFYC in Chicago. It fell to me to pick up on the momentum that Jeff had created. My job was essentially to continue the Chicago Youth Council and Day of Interfaith Youth Service projects; expand our network of relationships to include religious leaders, scholars, and journalists; and secure funding for the organization. I prayed for the day when working for the IFYC would be my full-time job. In the meantime, I took a faculty position at the Urban Studies Program, where I taught courses on religion to students from midwestern liberal arts colleges during a one-semester immersion in Chicago.

One of the first things I did was to call on Chicago's senior social movement leaders and intellectuals. For any new movement to be successful, it has to learn from effective movements of the past. Bill Ayers met me at 7:00 a.m. at the Gourmand café in the South Loop and gave me a jewel of advice: "Find the smaller stories that tell the larger story of your movement, and always begin with one of those."

I discovered that Martin Marty, one of America's most important scholars of religion, was speaking at a banquet one night. I bought a $60 ticket, stationed myself outside the banquet hall, and tapped him on the shoulder when he walked by. "Professor Marty, my name is Eboo Patel, and I'm starting an organization called the Interfaith Youth Core based largely on your theories of building religious pluralism," I said. "I paid $60 for a ticket to this banquet to be able to introduce myself to you. Will you give me a half hour of your time to tell you more?" A few weeks later, we met for an entire afternoon and talked about the importance of religious communities "risking hospitality" with one another. Hospitality became the first shared value for which the Interfaith Youth Core created a curriculum.

Ron Kinnamon, a former YMCA executive, saw an article about the IFYC in the *Chicago Tribune* and invited me to have lunch with him. We talked for several hours about the YMCA model of youth leadership development and the changes in America's religious demographics. "We in America know something about being a Judeo-Christian society, but we know nothing about living in a multifaith society," he said. "I think it's going to be young people who lead us into this new reality, and I think I just found the vanguard organization of that movement."

Mike Ivers, a former Catholic priest who ran a faith-based organization called Goodcity, saw the IFYC as next in line in the tradition of Chicago social justice movements. "Build the base of your organization here, buddy," he told me. "Once you get the model right, export it to the world stamped MADE IN CHICAGO." Goodcity served as a fiscal agent to Christian nonprofits, providing them with the necessary financial structure during their growing years. The IFYC was the first non-Christian organization Goodcity took on. "Interfaith work is Christ's work," Mike told his board members, who were a little nervous about the move. "This is the future of the church. This is the future of the city."

I visited Marjorie Benton, one of the most forward-thinking philanthropists in America, in her beautiful home in Evanston. "Don't neglect fundraising," she told me. "Money is the fuel of strong organizations. The earlier you build a funding base, the easier it will be for you as your organization grows." She had touched on the single most frustrating aspect of building the IFYC.

My initial forays into the foundation world had been entirely futile. Most program officers didn't return my phone calls or e-mails. When I finally set up a few meetings, I discovered how skilled program officers were at telling people no. They listened politely for a few minutes, then asked a set of questions that dealt with issues that were on their minds. For most of them, anything that dealt with religion was passé. They were part of the urban liberal school of thought that expected the Vatican to become Disneyland Rome soon. One told me that I needed a business plan to be taken seriously. Another suggested that I make a video of the programs the IFYC had run in India and South Africa to show to private donors. A third asked how the IFYC was engaging the issue of sexual orientation in our work. A fourth wanted to know whether we had a youth employment strategy.

None of them really paid attention to the big idea of the Interfaith Youth Core—the dream of young people building religious pluralism. We were immediately put into the box of soft human relations programs, the kind of thing that takes place in a junior high school cafeteria and involves PTA moms and camp songs. "You should just, you know, do local fundraising for your programs," one foundation person suggested as he ushered me out of his office.

I had a sudden urge to grab him by his suit jacket and say, "Do you think Osama bin Laden built Al Qaeda on bake sales?"

After months of frustration, I finally met a foundation person who saw the potential of the IFYC. Zahra Kassam, a young Muslim at the Ford Foundation with a degree from the Harvard Graduate School of Education, immediately understood the IFYC's vision and methodology. She asked smart questions about how the IFYC planned to go to scale and measure effectiveness. I sketched out my ideas on both issues, then decided to take a risk. "I feel like people at foundations are always asking questions designed to discourage me," I said. "Right now, the IFYC is a group of committed young adults who have run several effective interfaith youth projects around the world and are building a set of sustainable programs in Chicago. We would love to tell you we know exactly how to measure and scale our program, but how are we supposed to figure that out until we have the resources to properly run the program in the first place?"

Zahra was a program associate at the Ford Foundation, one of a group of talented recent college graduates who served primarily as research and support staff for the program officers. But Zahra's circle of program associates had their own ideas, too. They realized that Ford program officers tended to give grants to people and organizations with which they had some type of personal relationship. In fact, unless you ran a big-name organization, the only chance you had of getting a Ford Foundation grant was by getting the attention of a program officer. That meant either knowing the program officer directly or knowing someone who did.

The program associates, being younger, were constantly trying to get the program officers they worked for to support the artists and activists from their generation. But because the program officers did not know these people personally, the support rarely materialized. So the program associates approached a vice president at the Ford Foundation and requested their own pot of funding with the intention of making grants themselves. Thus was born the Emerging Voices, New Directions program. In the summer of 2002, Zahra called to tell me that the IFYC was being considered for a $35,000 grant from this fund.

I knew that this was a make-or-break opportunity for the IFYC, so I did what most nonprofit directors do when they are desperate: I over-promised. For $35,000, I told Zahra, the Interfaith Youth Core could teach a graduate-level course on the theory and practice of interfaith youth work and run a national conference that brought the leaders of various interfaith youth projects from across the country together to discuss best practices. These projects, I told Zahra, were crucial for our nascent field, and the IFYC had the knowledge base and networks to accomplish these tasks.

When the Ford Foundation grant was finalized, I rejoiced to my friend Joe Hall, and he gave me a golden piece of advice: a grant from a major foundation can be worth three times the amount of the actual check if you leverage it right. Sure enough, as soon as I told founda-tion program officers in Chicago that Ford was funding the IFYC, they paid attention in a whole new way. In a matter of months, we received grants from the Woods Fund of Chicago and the Chicago Community Trust. After two years of spinning our wheels in the funding world, we raised more than $100,000 in a few months.

Now we had to get the right team together. Because of my teaching job, I took only a small monthly stipend from the organization for the first year, and Jeff and I set out to look for a full-time staff person. Nei-ther of us had ever hired anybody, and we had no idea what criteria to use or how to go about the process. Thinking about the huge amount of work the IFYC had committed to, Jeff said to me, "Whoever we get better love our mission and never need to sleep."

In the end, she came to us. April Kunze had been involved in some of the young adult interfaith gatherings that Jeff had organized when he was first establishing the IFYC in Chicago. She had heard about an interfaith conference in Brazil and called to see if the IFYC could sponsor her to go.

"I know this is a strange request," she told Jeff when she called. "I mean, the last time I checked in on the IFYC, you had like $74 in your bank account."

Jeff arranged a meeting of the three of us, and one unlikely request was met with another. "Here's the deal," I told April. "The IFYC actually has some money now, and we can send you to this conference in Brazil, but there's one condition: you have to go as our staff member."

"I'm not sure I get what you are saying," she said slowly, looking closely at us to see if we were joking.

I told her about the Ford Foundation grant, the Chicago-based money that had followed, the huge task we had in front of us.

"Tell me more about the position you are hiring for," she said. "What's the job description?" She fired off a bunch of other questions about the "professional environment" and "opportunities for advancement." April clearly had more experience in these types of matters than either Jeff or I did.

We were at a bit of a loss. We hadn't really thought about any of those things. "Basically," Jeff told her, "you and Eboo are going to be responsible for running the projects and building the infrastructure of this organization. Eboo's the executive director, but he's got a full-time job teaching. So you are going to be carrying a lot of the load."

April left an excellent job with a foundation to become the IFYC's first full-time paid staff person, at 50 percent of her previous salary. It was, I believe, the luckiest break the IFYC has had in its organizational history. April brought an unbelievable range of skills to the IFYC. She created budgets, built bookshelves, wrote grant proposals, ran strategic planning sessions, hired and managed staff (and fired them when she needed to), designed youth programs, and kept spirits up. While I was off giving speeches, April was in the office creating a database to store the names I collected. When the media invitations started to roll in, April suggested devising a plan for how to use the media to build the interfaith youth movement. When I sent her a panicky midnight e-mail about a grant report that I had forgotten about, I got a 5:00 a.m. response saying that she had already turned it in.

She is that unique combination of brilliant visionary, team leader, and expert manager—a social entrepreneur in every sense of the word. When young executive directors of new nonprofits ask me for advice, I tell them this: find a number two who complements your skills and whom you would trust with your child. Give him or her anything he or she wants in terms of salary, title, and perks. Your organization can't survive without that person.

Even more than April's skills, it was her heart that made her a perfect fit for the IFYC. She was proud of being an Evangelical Christian, but she was uncomfortable with what that designation had come to mean in contemporary America. She had spent her Minnesota childhood singing praise songs, attending Bible camp, and going on missionary trips to Africa. Her mother had adopted several children out of a conviction that being Christian meant giving what you could to the less fortunate. The Kunze family was far from wealthy, but their home was safe and loving; their form of service was inviting people into it.

April went to Carleton College and was elected president of the campus Evangelical Christian group. She was on an e-mail list of religious leaders in Minnesota, and one day received a message from a Muslim imam in Minneapolis whose mosque had been burned down in a hate crime. The imam thought it would be a powerful statement if religious communities across Minnesota helped rebuild the mosque. April agreed. She began preparing for her campus group to raise money and volunteer for the effort, but several members rebelled. It was a sign of the divine that the mosque had burned down, they said, because it showed the Muslim community that God was displeased with their "devil worship," as one member put it. The task of the Christian at this time was to show these people the true path, not to help them rebuild their false shrine.

April could not believe her ears. She battled back but lost. She was deposed as president of the group. "If this is what being part of a Christian group is about, then I don't want it," April thought. She kept the light of Christ burning in her heart, but she refused to be involved in anything that had to do with organized Christianity. Instead, she threw herself fully into the work of social justice. When she graduated from college, she moved to Chicago and enrolled in Public Allies, a leadership program in which young people are placed as staff members in urban nonprofit organizations and engage in team-based community development projects. April quickly developed a reputation as a visionary with follow-through in Chicago's activist circles. She was hired as a senior staff member at a community development organization in one of Chicago's toughest neighborhoods and went about transforming its youth program, then creating a whole new youth organization called the Crib Collective.

But she felt that something was missing from her life: a community of faith. She discovered that pursuing social justice with only her private faith was an impossible path. She missed the church, but she was not willing to risk the rejection she had experienced from her fellow Christians when she had reached out to the Muslim community. After hearing Jeff talk about the Interfaith Youth Core, a space that connected faith, social justice, and diversity, she jumped at the chance to get involved. Her problem in the campus-based Christian group had been appearing not Christian enough as a result of her attempt to reach out to Muslims. Now she was worried that she would appear to be too Christian because she firmly believed that Christianity was a uniquely true religion and that Jesus was Lord and Savior. She confessed that worry during our initial interview. "I have the deepest respect for your faith," I told her. "I sure hope you think it's true, because otherwise there would be no reason to stay committed to it. I think my religion is true, too. So let's make a deal. We can both believe our religions are true, we can even privately hope the other converts, and we can work together in this organization to serve others. In that way, we, an Evangelical Christian and a devoted Muslim, can model what we say this organization is about: people from very different faith backgrounds finding common purpose in helping others."

———

In my first year as a teacher, I had a school director who had barely any experience in inner-city classrooms. Whenever she made a suggestion to the faculty about how to teach, we would roll our eyes and whisper, "If she had any ground-level experience in teaching, she wouldn't make so many stupid suggestions."

I realized how easily I could fall into that trap. I could spend all my time meeting with program officers and speaking on panels and never actually run any interfaith youth programs. I wouldn't get any personal experience of how the theories I was spouting worked in practice. I would make unreasonable demands on staff members who actually ran programs and give them advice that sounded good but had no traction. And sooner or later, people would say, "That guy doesn't know what he's talking about. He's never spent any real time actually doing the work." And they would be right. The principals that teachers respect the most are the ones who have been effective in the classroom and have an appreciation for what teaching really takes. Following that model, I decided I was going to be deeply involved with every one of the IFYC programs in the early stages of their development.

The first challenge was to get religious leaders on board. I met with people at the American Jewish Committee, the Catholic Archdiocese of Chicago, the Council of Islamic Organizations of Greater Chicago, and several other religious institutions. All of them were supportive of interfaith work in theory, and many had actually played a leadership role in adult interfaith programs, but they were universally apprehensive about involving their young people. "We barely have enough time to teach our kids about their *own* religion," they would say. "It's just not a high enough priority to spend that precious time exposing them to others." Underlying all of this seemed to be a suspicion that interfaith programs would somehow make other religions so alluring that there would be mass conversions, that hordes of young Jews would trade the message of Sinai for the lotus position and the Bodhi tree. After hearing this concern over and over again, I realized why most interfaith organizations could gather religious leaders but could not convince them to bring their youth groups: there is such a strong emphasis in most interfaith programs on collectively increasing spiritual peace and social justice that the importance of strengthening religious identity gets drowned out. Religious leaders are not particularly concerned about losing their own identities, so they do not consider involvement in interfaith work a threat to them. But they have a whole different set of concerns when it comes to their youth.

A senior person at the Archdiocese of Chicago put it like this: "I love the idea of interfaith cooperation. We certainly need more of that in this world. But my primary concern is that Catholic kids become better Catholics. I want them to know more about the Catholic tradition and to be more active in Catholic practices and institutions. Look, I think my religion has the banquet. I agree that all religions are holy and have something to offer, but I think Catholicism has the feast."

"I totally understand your position," I told him. "The truth is, most religious people feel that way. I certainly believe that Islam has something unique and powerful that holds my allegiance, and I believe one of my most important responsibilities as a Muslim is passing down my tradition to the next generation." I saw him easing a little bit in his chair. By proclaiming our strong commitment to our respective faiths, even intimating that we believed what we each had was superior, we had cleared the way for an honest conversation. Neither of us was offended by the other's faith commitment. To the contrary, it had created a common bond—two men of deep but different faiths talking about religious cooperation.

"The problem is that today's youths—Catholic, Muslim, Jewish, or whatever—no longer live in the so-called 'banquet hall' of their faith communities," I said. "They are coming into contact with kids from different backgrounds all the time. If they don't have a way of understanding how their faith relates to the Jews, Buddhists, Muslims, Hindus, Evangelicals, and others that they spend most of their lives around, then there's a good chance that their religious identities will atrophy."

He grew very attentive. I think he felt that I had put my finger on something important: how to maintain faith identity in a religiously plural world. I explained to him that one of the top priorities of the Interfaith Youth Core was to help young people strengthen their religious identities by creating a safe space where they could talk about faith.

"How do you make sure that they don't just argue about who is going to get into heaven?" he asked me.

"At the IFYC, we call those the 'mutually exclusive' discussions," I responded. "The truth is, our religious traditions have competing theological claims, and we simply have to accept those. There is little point in arguing about whether Hagar was Abraham's legitimate wife or his concubine, or whether it was Isaac or Ishmael on the rock. Even when we feel like we have found theological common ground—like Abraham as the patriarch of Jews, Christians, and Muslims—we quickly discover that even those paradigms have their limits. There are a million Hindus in this country, and over three million Buddhists, and neither of those communities would be called Abrahamic. But they live in America, too, and we have to have a paradigm that includes them."

"So what's the IFYC approach?"

"We call it shared values—service learning," I said. "We begin by identifying the values that different religious communities hold in common—hospitality, cooperation, compassion, mercy. We bring a group of religiously diverse young people together and ask them, 'How does your religion speak to this value?' One kid will say, 'Well, I really admire how the pope embodied mercy when he forgave the man who tried to assassinate him.' A kid from a different religion will say, 'There is a story like that in my religion: when the Prophet Muhammad returned to Mecca, he extended mercy by forgiving many of the people who had waged war against him.'"

"Are you trying to teach the kids that all religions are the same?" he asked, again growing suspicious.

"Not at all," I responded. "We are showing young people that religions have powerful things in common, but they come to those shared values through their own paths. Each religion has something unique to say about universal values through its particular set of scriptures, rituals, and heroes. This is a methodology that avoids the Scylla and Charybdis of interfaith work. The Scylla is the notion that we're all the same: I wash my hands before I pray; you wash your hands before you pray; everything else is details. We don't believe that's true. We believe the differences between religions are extremely important. As a devout Muslim, I certainly want to preserve the uniqueness of my religion. But you can go too far in that direction, right into the jaws of Charybdis, which is the thinking that religious differences are so great that we can't even talk. The middle path, the only route to collective survival really, is to identify what is common between religions but to create the space where each can articulate its distinct path to that place. I think of it as affirming particularity and achieving pluralism."

The Catholic leader sighed. "I've got to admit, it sounds great in theory," he told me. "I'm just afraid kids today don't know enough about their own religions to be able to tell the stories that you expect from them."

"I did my doctorate on religious education programs. One of my biggest discoveries was that kids know a lot more about their religions than their teachers think. It's a matter of what kind of space you create and how you ask the questions. That's why the IFYC always gives young people the chance to actually act on the religious value they are talking about through a service project. It's amazing how many faith stories of compassion kids remember when they are building a house together for a poor family, or what their insights into hospitality are when they are tutoring refugee children."

I had much the same conversation at the American Jewish Committee, Greek Orthodox Metropolis of Chicago, Catholic Theological Union, Lutheran School of Theology, Chicago Theological Seminary, and Council of Islamic Organizations of Greater Chicago. Once these various religious leaders felt assured that the IFYC had a sense of how precious religious identity is and had a methodology that

both preserved their own religion's particularity while building interfaith understanding, they were happy to give me the names of con-
tacts in their communities who worked with teenagers. These leads
were generally my peers—well-educated professionals in their twenties who volunteered as religious education teachers and youth advisers. I would explain that Emily Soloff at the American Jewish
Committee or Father Demetri at the Greek Orthodox Metropolis had
suggested I call about getting their youth involved in a new interfaith
service program. I would give them the background and methodology
of the Interfaith Youth Core and ask them whether they had young
people who wanted to participate in our Chicago Youth Council. Inevitably, they would say, "Why don't you come to one of my youth
meetings and ask them yourself."

And so I spent a lot of time in the basements of synagogues,
churches, and mosques, telling teenagers about the Interfaith Youth
Core. I was prepared for reactions ranging from skepticism to teenage boredom. Instead, I received almost unanimous enthusiasm. "You
mean, we do projects together with kids from different religions and
talk about our own faith and listen to them talk about theirs?" a high
schooler at the Muslim Education Center asked me.

"That's basically it," I said.

"Man, what a cool idea," she said with a smile.

I thought back to my own high school experience, and how faith
was the one topic that we didn't talk about at the lunch table because
none of us knew how. I realized that these kids were excited about the
Interfaith Youth Core because it was giving them a space and a language to talk openly about something that was such a big part of their
lives but was too often hidden from others.

It did not take long to find eight young people to become the
2002–2003 Interfaith Youth Core Chicago Youth Council.

The CYC met on Monday afternoons at St. Ignatius Catholic Church
in Rogers Park. I bought kosher snacks on the way to meetings, drove

kids home afterward, and prepared interfaith homework assignments such as "Find a faith hero in your tradition who exemplifies the shared value of hospitality and make a five-minute presentation on him or her next week." Each year the CYC chose a service project where the members could put their shared values into action. One year it was working with homeless people; another year it was tutoring refugee children. The students would do the service project one week, then go through a guided interfaith dialogue the following week. When Mariah Neuroth took over the CYC in 2003–2004, she added a new dimension: at the end of every year, the CYC created an art project that embodied the group's interfaith service learning experience. The year they worked with homeless people, they made a video scrapbook on different religious ideas of home. The year they worked with refugee kids, they wrote a children's book that wove religious motifs through a refugee's story.

The CYC was where I saw the IFYC theory come to life. I watched devout kids from different religions deepen both their own faith and their relationships with others. I was astounded by how theologically insightful young people could be during interfaith discussions. A Muslim participant asked a Christian why his church collected gifts for needy families at Christmas. "Well," the Christian responded, "Christmas commemorates the birth of Jesus, who was a gift to us, a people who needed spiritual guidance. The best way for us to celebrate Christmas is to follow the example of Jesus and try to provide gifts for the people around us."

I watched the CYC members become interfaith youth leaders. They were interviewed about interfaith youth work on television and radio programs. They made speeches to gatherings of hundreds of other teenagers about the importance of building religious pluralism. And on more than one occasion, I watched them intervene when adult interfaith groups began drifting into useless theological and political disagreement, bringing them back to constructive discussions based on shared values.

The IFYC also continued to run the Day of Interfaith Youth Service program, bringing hundreds of religiously diverse young people from across the Chicago area together for a day of volunteering and interfaith dialogue. A group of curious religious leaders and parents always tagged along. "I wanted to come see why my child has been so interested in religion lately," one said. "A year ago, I couldn't force her to go to Hebrew school. Now she can't wait to go. She keeps telling me that she has to learn more about Judaism so she can have more to say at the Day of Interfaith Youth Service."

I could not help but think back to all the adult interfaith programs I had been to, which always promised that the youth program would follow once the adults built trusting relationships. "When are the kids coming?" I would ask.

"Next week," they would tell me.

It turns out that the opposite logic was true. If you center the interfaith program around young people, the adults and religious leaders inevitably show up.

Even though the Day of Interfaith Youth Service was a one-time, short-term event, it had a catalytic effect because entire youth groups would participate and return to their community with a whole set of questions about their own religion and how it relates to the faith of others. Watching eighty Muslims perform the late-afternoon salat caused a group of Jews to wonder whether their religion had an afternoon prayer practice. They discovered that Judaism did have such a ritual, called Mincha.

After the 2004 Day of Interfaith Youth Service, the students at the Universal Muslim School, a largely Arab American institution located in a suburb just south of Chicago, started an afterschool group to study Muslim texts that speak to religious pluralism. They also tripled their participation in the school's volunteer program. "The Day of Service changed their whole lives," one of their teachers told me. "So many parts of it were new to them: that there were other

Americans who were religious, too; that Islam has such a strong tradition of pluralism and service; that they had so much in common
with Jews and Christians. They were truly never the same again."

The first National Conference on Interfaith Youth Work was held
at the University of Chicago in 2003 and attended by some forty people, including college professors and chaplains, student interfaith activists, and Chicago-area religious leaders. Each participant presented
a paper on his or her own interfaith youth program: the research-based
Pluralism Project at Harvard University led by Grove Harris and Diana Eck; the interfaith student council that Victor Kazanjian had established at Wellesley College; Joe Hall's program in the South Bronx
that brought Catholic and Pentecostal kids together to make films on
sacred journeys; the E Pluribus Unum interfaith summer camp created
by Sid Schwarz. By the end of the conference, we discovered that
nearly twenty different projects were represented in the room. "All
this time, I thought that I was the only person doing this work," one
person said, a hint of shock in her voice. Anastasia White had been
right. There was something so resonant in the idea of interfaith youth
cooperation that it had emerged independently in many places at
once and was beginning to take a variety of expressions. We had the
chance to turn this into a movement. The challenge was to create a
spread strategy and a strong network.

We decided that the papers needed to be collected into a book,
which we called *Building the Interfaith Youth Movement* (published in
2006). Melodye Feldman of the Denver-based organization Building
Bridges for Peace suggested that the growing interfaith youth movement needed an annual conference. Others agreed. Somebody else
pointed out that we needed one common program that everyone
did together. I talked about our Day of Interfaith Youth Service in
Chicago. Julie Eberly said she ran a similar project at Interfaith Ministries for Greater Houston. "That's the one," said Patrice Brodeur, a
longtime supporter of interfaith youth programs. And so the Day of

Interfaith Youth Service was born, first as a national program and now as a global one.

A book, an annual conference, a national program: "Who is going to coordinate all of these things?" I asked. All eyes turned to me. "Does that answer your question?" Patrice said.

Overnight, the IFYC had picked up a national brief. The pebble had been kicked off the mountain, and it was beginning to gather speed.

Shehnaz's mother swears that she knew we were going to get married the first time she saw us together. Her family is from the same part of India as mine, Gujarat, land of merchants and mustaches. They practice the Sufi-tinged interpretation of Islam common to Gujarat: put a black dot on the lucky person to ward off the evil eye, visit the graves of Muslim saints for blessings, chant the shahada when the moon comes out. It has strong similarities to the Ismaili understanding of Islam. From the start, Shehnaz was very comfortable around Ismailis. She liked that the community was both unabashedly modern and devoutly Muslim; that so many of the women were professionals and in positions of community leadership; that we were putting so many resources into nurturing Islam's cultural and intellectual heritage, from Middle Eastern architecture to Central Asian music. She sat with me while I prayed the Ismaili Du'a and always expressed great admiration for the work of the Imam.

One night, at dinner, I asked whether Shehnaz was interested in taking the next step. "I mean, your practice of Islam is so similar to the Ismaili understanding. Plus, don't you think it would make things easier, in the future and all?"

She gave me a look that said I had made two missteps. The lesser crime was suggesting we were going to get married without properly asking. "There's no romance in insinuations. When you're ready to do it, do it right, and pray that the answer is yes," she told me flatly.

Second, and far more serious, she didn't appreciate my telling her what her religion was. It was true, she felt a deep resonance with parts of the Ismaili tariqa, but there was also a disconnect. "I didn't grow up with the notion of an Imam. My family believes in the message of the Qur'an and the life and teachings of the Prophet, and the way those became spiritually embedded in India. It's actually not a small step to adopt the Ismaili position. It's like a Protestant becoming a Catholic and adding to her belief in Jesus and the Bible the idea and authority of the pope."

I was supposedly the professional in matters of religious identity and diversity, but Shehnaz had clearly thought about this issue more intelligently than I had. It was important to both of us to be with a person who shared the same language of prayer. Shehnaz was reminding me that there were multiple dialects within a language, and those differences needed to be respected within the unity of the broader tradition. She pointed me to a saying of the Prophet: "Differences within my community are a mercy."

I wondered how my parents would react. My dad, typically, said he was thrilled I was getting married and, frankly, not a little surprised. My mother, also typically, got tears in her eyes, hugged me and Shehnaz, and said she loved us both.

Finally, there was the issue of Mama, in Bombay. Since I was eight years old, she had made me promise to marry an Ismaili. Mama had guided me back to the faith. She was the last person I wanted to disappoint.

I took Shehnaz to see her a few months before the wedding. I asked my father to tell her that Shehnaz was a Muslim, but not an Ismaili. I was too scared to break the news to her myself. My grandmother had always drawn from the broader Muslim tradition but insisted that we marry Ismailis. When we arrived on her doorstep in Bombay, Mama greeted us with smiles and kisses. She asked us to sit on her special sofa and put garlands of flowers around our necks. "I am so happy you two are getting married," she said. "To my grandson, Eboo, Ya Ali Madad," the Ismaili greeting meaning "May Ali help you."

"And to my new granddaughter, beautiful, precious Shehnaz, As-salamu Alaikum," the more general Muslim greeting meaning "Peace be upon you."

"May Allah bless this union."

Farid Esack, a South African Muslim leader, officiated at our marriage ceremony, drawing in both Sunni and Ismaili elements. Kevin gave the best man's speech. Jeff said the blessing over the food. I thought, "This is forever," as I put on Shehnaz's finger a ring inscribed with a line from Pablo Neruda: "Rest with your dream in my dream."

Conclusion:
Saving Each Other,
Saving Ourselves

> My heart has grown capable of taking on all forms
> It is a pasture for gazelles
> A table for the Torah
> A convent for Christians
> Ka'bah for the Pilgrim
> Whichever the way love's caravan shall lead
> That shall be the way of my faith.
>
> IBN ARABI

"My dear brothers and sisters, Assalamu Alaikum. I come to you in this beautiful house of worship with the Muslim greeting of peace." It was February 2004, and I was listening to Imam Feisal Abdul Rauf give the Sunday sermon at New York City's Riverside Church. He talked about Islam as a tradition meant for all places and times, a faith that had sustained billions of followers for more than a thousand years and contributed enormous quantities of beauty to human civilization. Imam Feisal wore a traditional white robe from the Middle East, and his accent bore the traces of his past: the Arab world, Malaysia, England. But his message was about the here and now. In that church where Martin Luther King Jr. had given his famous speech against the Vietnam War, Imam Feisal talked about the emergence of a twenty-first-century American Islam.

I approached Imam Feisal after his sermon and told him about the Interfaith Youth Core. He understood the vision immediately and suggested that I visit him and his wife, Daisy Khan, at their home the following evening. The living room of their apartment on the Upper West Side was set up like a mosque, with prayer rugs stretched from wall to wall. I arrived at dusk. We said the Maghrib prayer, then talked about how America, with its unique combination of religious devotion and religious diversity, was the ideal place for a renewal of Islam. "In the twentieth century, Catholicism and Judaism underwent profound transformations in America," Imam Feisal observed. "I think this century, in America, Islam will do the same." Imam Feisal said that it was young American Muslims, a generation both unabashedly American and unmistakably Muslim, who would shape American Islam. And he hoped that my generation in America could reach out to our peers across the Muslim world, approximately 70 percent of whom were under thirty years old, and we could renew Islam together.

Islam is a religion that has always been revitalized by migration. The waters of the faith, says one scholar, are so clear that they pick up the colors of the rocks they flow over. Islam in India looks Indian; in China, Chinese. The cultural tradition of contemporary Islam owes enormous debts to Indian architecture, Persian cuisine, Turkish poetry, Arabic calligraphy, and Greek philosophy. What colors will America add to Islam?

America is a nation that has been constantly rejuvenated by immigrants. For centuries, they have added new notes to the American song. There is now a critical mass of Muslims in America. About 75 percent are people who undertook a geographic migration, coming from South Asia, the Middle East, and various parts of Africa. Approximately 25 percent were born in the United States, mostly African Americans, who chose the spiritual migration of conversion. Most estimates put the total population of Muslims in America at six million, about the same as the number of Jews and almost triple the number of Episcopalians. What notes will Islam contribute to the American song?

Imam Feisal introduced me to a community answering both questions at once. At the Muslim Leaders of Tomorrow conference that he and Daisy convened in the spring of 2004, I met the best of my generation of Muslims: artists and bankers, African American converts and Middle Eastern immigrants, Sunnis and Shias, women who wore headscarves and women who didn't. We woke up early to do Sufi chants with Imam Feisal, had heated debates over how best to participate in American politics, and rolled off our chairs laughing at the act of the Muslim comedian Azhar Usman. Three themes emerged in the discussion: Islam had to be a big tent for all believers, not a small room for only the purists; Muslims needed to contribute to all aspects of human civilization, not obsess exclusively over a handful of causes; and American Muslims needed to be just as concerned with the future of the country we lived in as we were about the places of Islam's glorious past.

I had grown up comfortable with diversity but unclear about my identity. Finally, I had found a community I could call my own.

Jen had the opposite experience. Her parents wanted her to have a strong Jewish identity, so they raised her entirely within a Jewish bubble. She grew up in a Jewish neighborhood, attended a Jewish school, and went to Jewish summer camps. One day, at a restaurant, Jen grew visibly upset around a dark-skinned employee. Her mother realized that Jen's discomfort was based on her limited contact with non-Jews, and that if Jen was going to make her way in a diverse world, she needed to come out of the Jewish cocoon. How to do that while maintaining a strong Jewish identity? Jen's parents hoped the Interfaith Youth Core's Chicago Youth Council would help.

Sayyeda, a young woman from a traditional Muslim family, joined the CYC at about the same time Jen did. I watched them, a devout Jew and a devout Muslim, each raised in the bubble of her own community, slowly come to know each other. They built their relationship by volunteering together—tutoring children, spending time with senior citizens, painting the walls of community centers. After a particularly challenging afternoon with refugee children on the North Side of Chicago, I saw Sayyeda recite to Jen Sura Asr from the Qur'an, about the importance of staying patient while doing good work. During an interfaith discussion on the importance of teachers in different religions, Jen talked about a famous Jewish scholar named Rashi and how he gave his daughters the same duties as his sons. I could see Sayyeda's mind working on that idea. She had spent the past several years thinking about gender issues within Islam, and hearing Jen point to Rashi had made her curious about whether Islam had a similar teacher. They also had several lighter moments together. Before leading a discussion on shared values between religious communities at the Catholic Theological Union, they slipped away to the restroom together, then came out laughing hysterically. "What's so funny?" I asked. They had been trading the prayers that Jews and Muslims say while using the bathroom.

"Honestly, it's like talking to another Muslim," Sayyeda said of their friendship. "I have the same relationship with Jen as I do with some of my Muslim friends. I find that kind of ironic."

Jen nodded. "Anyone spiritual goes through very similar struggles in their lives. Would I go to Sayyeda to talk about how to practice modesty? Absolutely, because she's exemplary in her modesty. Even if we have different traditions, we still grapple with the same ideas."

One of the ideas that Jen and Sayyeda both grappled with was being committed to your own tradition while empathizing with another person's perspective. During one CYC meeting, Sayyeda confessed, "It seems like most of my life I've only been looking at one side. I'm struggling with this idea of seeing both sides. I've been opened up to these new cultures, these new faiths, new people. I guess it's better to open up the lid in a box than to just close it." She explained that she had not gone to a protest on behalf of Palestine because she didn't feel as if concrete solutions were offered and she didn't feel right about just denouncing something.

Jen's eyes flipped wide open as she listened to Sayyeda. "I was invited to go to the anti-protest to that Palestinian rally. And as much as I support Israel, never would I go and protest someone else, and it's probably out of a direct relationship with you," she said, gesturing to Sayyeda.

"See, yeah, that's it," Sayyeda said. "I used to look at a newspaper and see a heading that says, 'Palestinian Terrorist Blows Himself Up.' And as sad as this sounds, I could understand why. But now, it seems like there are much better alternatives than to turn to violence."

"We had a really pro-Israeli event at my Jewish youth group, and somebody told the story of an Islamic leader being assassinated and people started clapping," Jen said. "I was about to stand up and say, 'What are you doing? That's a human life. You can't clap when somebody dies.'" She choked back tears, then continued. "I find myself in every situation arguing the opposite side, because now I know you and I see both sides."

"Same here," said Sayyeda.

We talked about the Muslim concept of being a mercy upon all the world. Jen brought up the saying of the first-century Palestinian rabbi Hillel: "If I am not for myself, who will be for me? If I am only for myself, what am I?" Understanding the other person's point of view, we determined, was a core value in both Islam and Judaism.

To see the other side, to defend another people, not despite your tradition but because of it, is the heart of pluralism. It is this same ethic that I see exemplified in the Indian art film Mr. and Mrs. Iyer. It is about a young Muslim photographer and a young Hindu housewife who come from very different backgrounds and have very different temperaments but find themselves on the same cross-country bus. The bus stalls in a part of the country where riots are raging. Muslim and Hindu mobs are roaming the area and murdering people of the other religion. A group of extremist Hindus climb aboard the bus and start checking IDs. They murder the ones with Muslim names. When they approach the young Muslim photographer, the Hindu woman stops them and says that he is her husband. The two finally escape the Hindu extremists on the bus and make it to a nearby village, only to find themselves in the midst of a group of Muslim extremists. The photographer risks his life to protect the woman and the baby, claiming that they are his own.

I saw the film in a theater in Bombay. I thought about the times when my family there had to lock themselves in their home for fear of the raging Hindu and Muslim mobs on the streets of their city. I thought about my own failure to protect my Jewish friend in high school when people had targeted his religion for ridicule. I thought about what the young religious extremists we read about in the news every day could have been if different influences had gotten to them first. I thought about the meaning of pluralism in a world where the forces that seek to divide us are strong. I came to one conclusion: We have to save each other. It's the only way to save ourselves.

Postscript

Post proofs that brotherhood
is not so wild a dream as those who profit
by postponing it pretend.

NORMAN CORWIN

Movements re-create the world.

A movement is a growing group of people who believe so deeply in a new possibility that they participate in making it a reality. They won't all meet. They won't even know everybody else's names. But somehow, they all have the feeling that people on the other side of the city or the country or the world believe in the same idea, burn with the same passion, and are taking risks for the same dream.

This book is the story of how I came to participate in the movement of religious pluralism. Everywhere I go—from villages outside Kandy, Sri Lanka, to community centers in Amman, Jordan, to offices at the State Department in Washington, D.C.—I find people with a similar story. When thousands of people discover that their story is also someone else's story, they have the chance to write a new story together.

The purpose of the Interfaith Youth Core is to catalyze, provide resources for, and network with the growing international interfaith youth movement. If you have been doing interfaith projects for years, we want to learn from your model. If you believe deeply in the vision of religious pluralism but do not know where to start, we want to provide you with resources to get going. If you teach at a school or in a religious education program and need answers to questions about how Islam (or any other religion) calls on its followers to cooperate with others to serve the world, we have materials that might help. The Interfaith Youth Core has produced activity guides on how to run interfaith service projects and academic papers on how to think about some of the thorniest issues in interfaith work. We hold annual conferences in Chicago and send speakers and trainers to campuses and communities around the world. Come visit us on our website, and let's see how we can work together.

"I'm not really religious," a high school junior in Mercersburg, Pennsylvania, told me, "but I want to be a part of this."

"We need you," I said.

The question of the faith line cannot be answered by drawing a line between the religious and the nonreligious. Pluralism—even religious pluralism—is everybody's business, for both the obvious pragmatic reasons and the more poetic ones. After all, there are many places where people hear the music of transcendence. To paraphrase Bob Dylan, some folks find the beyond in the church of their choice, some folks find it in a Woody Guthrie song.

We need all of those people—the hymn singers and the sun saluters, the Qur'an reciters and the mandala makers, the speakers of Hebrew and the readers of Sanskrit, the hip-hop heads and the folk music fans—and more. We need a language that allows us to emphasize our unique inspirations and affirm our universal values. We need spaces where we can each state that we are proud of where we came from and all point to the place we are going to.

I fear the road is long. I rejoice that we travel together.

Afterword

> we are each other's
> harvest:
> we are each other's
> business:
> we are each other's
> magnitude and bond.
>
> GWENDOLYN BROOKS

When the first black president of the United States spoke of identity in his inaugural address, he used these words:

> For we know that our patchwork heritage is a strength, not a weakness. We are a nation of Christians and Muslims, Jews and Hindus —and non-believers. . . . We cannot help but believe that the old hatreds shall someday pass; that the lines of tribe shall soon dissolve; that as the world grows smaller, our common humanity shall reveal itself; and that America must play its role in ushering in a new era of peace.

I was there that day, standing on the National Mall with over one million of my favorite citizens, astonished by Obama's language.

It was the urgency with which he spoke of religious diversity that got me. During the campaign Obama had been exalted for shattering racial barriers and hounded for the Muslim faith of his grandfather. I wouldn't have been surprised if he had avoided the topic of religion in his inaugural address altogether. Instead, he put the issue center stage, making it crystal clear that bridging the faith divide was going to be one of the priorities of his presidency.

A few weeks later, I got a phone call from the White House. Joshua Dubois, director of the White House Office of Faith-based and Neighborhood Partnerships, started the conversation with the word "congratulations." Obama had appointed me to the twenty-five-member Faith Council, and the president wanted to meet with us later that week. When the Faith Council gathered in the Oval Office that Thursday morning, the president wasted little time getting down to business.

Our formal task, he said, was to deliver at the end of one year a set of recommendations about how the federal government could better partner with faith and community-based organizations in several areas, including reducing poverty, strengthening families, improving the environment, and advancing interfaith cooperation.

I was thrilled that interfaith cooperation was an explicit priority area, but I got an even better sense of how the president viewed this issue when he grew reflective and started talking about his broader vision for the role of diverse faith communities in our society. He said he hoped that religious communities would expand their service and community-building programs at this time of economic crisis, and repeated a sentence from his National Prayer Breakfast address: "The particular faith that motivates each of us can promote a greater good for all of us." Such social-action efforts, he noted, could illustrate the shared values between diverse religious communities and thus provide common ground for interfaith dialogue and understanding. Finally, the president spoke of the idealism and energy of young people, and said that we should be especially mindful of engaging the leadership of the next generation in faith-based social action and interfaith co-operation.

At this point, my friend and mentor Jim Wallis of Sojourners, one of the other members of the Faith Council, leaned over and whispered in my ear, "It sounds like the president has read the mission statement of the Interfaith Youth Core." It sure did, and I couldn't believe my ears.

As the meeting was winding down, the president asked if there were any final questions or comments. I decided it was now or never. "Mr. President, what you were saying earlier about faith and service, diversity and common ground, young people showing leadership in social action and interfaith cooperation—my organization, the Interfaith Youth Core, is trying to build a global movement out of that very energy. Thank you for sharing our vision."

Obama smiled that megawatt smile—it looked even better in person than it did on TV—and said: "We'll be following up with you on that." And follow up he did, from dedicating a week of the United We Serve campaign to interfaith service efforts to making interfaith cooperation a theme of his historic Cairo address. The grassroots interfaith youth movement had gotten a global stage.

I wrote *Acts of Faith* when the Interfaith Youth Core was just getting off the ground. I can't help but smile as I reread the book now and think back to those early days of the organization. Our first leadership program involved eight young people meeting weekly in the basement of a Catholic church in Rogers Park, Illinois. Our early university-based training programs engaged a few dozen students—total—from Penn, Illinois, Northwestern, and DePaul. Our first national conference drew forty people. I spent a lot of weekends driving long distances to speak to gatherings of twenty-five or thirty people. We were overjoyed when a local media outlet did a short feature on IFYC, thinking it was our one shot at getting the message out to a larger audience. Funding was so precarious that I talked to my wife

more than once about the possibility of having to forego a few pay-
checks. In short, the IFYC was a fledgling organization dreaming of a
grassroots movement.

We've come a long way. Our most recent conference drew 650
people, including delegations from a dozen countries. The Chicago
Youth Council has morphed into a national Fellows Alliance program
for exceptional college students who are transforming their campuses
into models of interfaith cooperation. We've added an international
fellowship called FaithsAct, a partnership with the Tony Blair Faith
Foundation, which involves thirty recent college graduates dedicating a year to building interfaith alliances focused on ending deaths related to malaria. The IFYC now has a team of speakers and trainers;
we're more likely to be in front of an audience of 250 than 25, and
we occasionally find ourselves addressing upwards of 2,500 people.
We are regular contributors to national and global media, including
the *Washington Post, National Public Radio,* and *CNN,* and have been
featured on several high-profile programs, including *Good Morning
America.* Over the last few years, major philanthropists have made
significant investments in the IFYC, and we've also managed to build
a fee-for-service dimension into our work, allowing us to grow our staff
to over thirty full-time professionals at the time of this writing.

What's even more impressive than the growth of the Interfaith
Youth Core is the emergence of a genuine grassroots interfaith youth
movement. Cities like St. Paul, Philadelphia, Los Angeles, Seattle,
and Sharon, Massachusetts, have interfaith youth programs, and I
hear of several more communities every month that are in the process
of launching their own. Campuses from Berea College in Kentucky
and Luther College in Iowa to Stanford, Princeton, and Yale have all
made interfaith cooperation a high priority. Graduates of Interfaith
Youth Core programs are making their mark as well, winning pres-
tigious scholarships like the Mitchell and the Truman, launching academic journals with a focus on interfaith cooperation, starting their
own interfaith nonprofit organizations, and using their interfaith

leadership skills to advance issues related to food justice and public health.

So how does an emerging movement best utilize the opportunity of the global stage? I think we start by articulating a big, bold vision —the kind of vision that a lot of folks may think is out of reach. And then we put forth a strategy that makes believers out of skeptics and leaders out of believers. So here's the big, bold vision: interfaith cooperation should be a social norm, the same way that environmentalism, human rights, multiculturalism, and volunteerism are social norms. We'll know that interfaith cooperation is getting there when we simply expect houses of worship to be involved in regular interfaith service projects, just like they do regular Habitat for Humanity projects now; when it's just the status quo for cities to host a Day of Interfaith Youth Service program and thousands of people come, including the mayor; when college campuses make a commitment to being models of interfaith cooperation; and when religious prejudice is challenged with the same frequency and intensity that racial bigotry is called out.

And here's the Interfaith Youth Core strategy. First, be aggressive about spreading the vision of interfaith cooperation. Religious extremists and religious bigots are not shy about shouting their ideas from the mountaintops, and we need to compete with and ultimately defeat their message machines. We are building a top-notch communications department at IFYC with the goal of using every channel available to us—from college newspapers to CNN, from websites to the White House bully pulpit—to advance the idea that this century needs to be characterized by bridges between different faith communities, not bombs. Second, help higher education become a model of interfaith cooperation. Campuses already have a religiously diverse student body, a commitment to civic engagement and student leadership, and a desire to be at the vanguard of important social change. Just as college campuses have become models of multiculturalism and environmentalism, with concrete goals they commit to achieving, they can also become models of interfaith cooperation. The IFYC wants to work with five hundred campuses over the next several years to help them advance toward this goal. Third, we want to inspire, train, and mobilize a critical mass of young people as interfaith leaders. This was the animating vision of the IFYC from the beginning, and it remains a cornerstone today. Interfaith leaders have the vision, the knowledge base, and the skill set to change negative conversations about religious diversity into positive ones, to launch sustainable interfaith cooperation projects, and to transform environments (their home, their college campus, their city) into models of interfaith cooperation.

A hundred years ago the terms "environmentalist" or "human rights activist" were not broadly recognized in our culture; they were social roles that evolved as societies grew more concerned with our effects on the earth and came to accept the idea that there are basic rights that any human being should be afforded. As we increasingly come to understand the importance of interfaith understanding and cooperation, the Interfaith Youth Core hopes to make the term "interfaith leader" a new identity category in our culture, something that idealistic young people aspire to become. Ultimately, it is going to be a generation of interfaith leaders who make interfaith cooperation a social norm. Our job at the Interfaith Youth Core is to catalyze, resource, and network this generation of interfaith leaders, and watch them change the world.

Acknowledgments

This is a book painfully penned by one set of hands and proudly carrying the fingerprints of many, many others. Thank you to Bill Ayers for suggesting that there may be a story worth telling floating around in my head, and for introducing me to the fantastic people at Beacon Press. A special thanks to my Beacon editor, Amy Caldwell, who may have spent more time on repairs for this manuscript than on any other book she has edited. The support provided by Swanee Hunt, James Jensen, Aaron Olver, and Ron Kinnamon made this book both easier and more fun to write. Thank you to Cecelia Weiss, Nick Price, and Erin Williams for helping me with the research for this book. Thanks to Hussein Rashid, Jane Rechtman, Jeff Pinzino, Jennifer Zlotow, Roy Bahat, and Reza Aslan for reviewing the manuscript with care and providing valuable insights. This book is very much the product of conversations with the staff, the board, and all the young people of the Interfaith Youth Core, as well as my colleagues in the broader interfaith movement. It is a tribute to their vision, energy, and friendship.

My mom, dad, and brother have always provided the right balance of challenge and support for all of my crazy endeavors. I thank them for bringing the same love to this book. And finally, thanks to my wife, Shehnaz Mansuri, who embodies in human form so many of the central values of the Muslim tradition—compassion, mercy, patience, and constancy—and who read draft after draft, corrected the major errors, allowed the minor ones, and stayed my best friend and key co-conspirator throughout.

Bibliographic Essay

This is a book, like so many of the characters within it, that lives at the intersection of many fields, movements, and archetypes: terrorists and faith heroes, religious totalitarianism and religious pluralism, social entrepreneurship and academic theory, current events and ancient traditions, the Harlem of life and the Heavens of thought. Its sources are equally diverse. Many of them are embedded in the text. The purpose of this essay is to give the reader a sense of where some of the more specific material I cite comes from and to suggest avenues for additional reading.

For current events, I generally relied on well-regarded newspapers and periodicals, including the *New York Times*, *The New Yorker*, *Foreign Affairs*, the *New York Review of Books*, and *The Atlantic Monthly*. For information on the London Tube bombings, I also used several British sources, including the *Guardian*, the *Independent*, the BBC, and the British government's official report on the bombings. My information on Eric Rudolph came largely from the *New York Times* reports of his capture and his trials and from a book called *Hunting Eric Rudolph* by Henry Schuster with Charles Stone.

I tell some specific stories about religious violence in this book. My main source on Hindu nationalism in India is an excellent report titled *The Foreign Exchange of Hate*. My source on Yossi Klein Halevi's story of becoming a Jewish extremist at the hands of Meir Kahane is his autobiography, *Memoirs of a Jewish Extremist*. The quotes in chapter 7 come from this book.

There are several excellent books on the causes of religious violence. For information on the roots of Muslim violence, Al Qaeda, and September 11, I found *The Looming Tower* by Lawrence Wright, *Perfect Soldiers* by Terry McDermott, *Landscapes of the Jihad* by Faisal Devji, and *Messages to the World: The Statements of Osama bin Laden* by Bruce Lawrence particularly useful. For books on the more general issue of religious violence, I like Karen Armstrong's *The Battle for God*, Jessica Stern's *Terror in the Name of God*, Mark Jurgensmeyer's *Terror in the Mind of God*, Martin Marty's *When Faiths Collide*, and Martin Marty and Scott Appleby's *The Glory and the Power*, an accessible book based on their multivolume Fundamentalism Project.

There are two industries working overtime to produce bad books about Islam: Muslim extremists and Islamophobes. What a better world it would be if these groups all went into one room and read one another's books. (If they stayed away from their guns long enough, they might even realize how similar their visions actually are.) Thankfully, there are also many excellent books on Islam. My personal favorites include *Major Themes of the Qur'an* by Fazlur Rahman; *No god but God* by Reza Aslan; *What's Right with Islam Is What's Right with America* by Imam Feisal Abdul Rauf; *Qur'an, Liberation and Pluralism* by Farid Esack; and *Muhammad* by Karen Armstrong. As I stated in chapter 1, the United States is blessed to have a number of exceptional Muslim scholars who are steeped in the Muslim tradition and are committed to the project of pluralism in America and beyond. The most senior of this group is Dr. Umar Abd-Allah, the scholar in residence of the Nawawi Foundation in Chicago. The importance of his essays cannot be overstated. Not only have they awakened many a young Muslim to the beauty of his faith, but they also provide the intellectual architecture for a twenty-first-century Islam that remains the roots of the tradition and seeks not only to acculturate but also to contribute to it. These essays include "Islam Cultural Imperative," "Mercy, the Stamp of Creation," and

"Innovation and Creativity in Islam." They can be found at the Nawawi Foundation website. For more on the Aga Khan, the Aga Khan Development Network, and the Ismaili community, see the websites of the Institute of Ismaili Studies and the Aga Khan Development Network.

Underlying this book are both theories of religion and theories of pluralism. My favorite theories of religion can be found in two short books. Wilfred Cantwell Smith's *The Faith of Other Men* was written in the early 1960s, at a time when America was finally accepting the presence of Jews and Catholics, and many years before it would become aware of growing Muslim, Hindu, and Buddhist communities. As if looking into a crystal ball, Smith stated, "The religious life of mankind from now on, if it is to be lived at all, will be lived in a context of religious pluralism." He was cautiously optimistic about this prospect, but warned that it would require a massive shift in religious understanding, particularly from his fellow Christians, who would have to learn to see the faith of other people as just as deeply rooted and genuine as their own. Smith called for a field of inquiry that focuses not so much on religious systems as religious people—in other words, more concerned with understanding how Buddhists and Christians will live together than with whether Buddhism and Christianity have theological points in common. My other favorite book in the theory of religion is Aziz Esmail's *The Poetics of Religious Experience*, which uses examples from Islam to illustrate that religions are best understood as traditions with a core essence that communities of believers interpret and give expression to in a range of ways across time and place. The essential vision of Islam can be stated simply as submission to the will of God—a core idea shared by Muslims from tenth-century North Africa to twenty-first-century North America, but understood and put into practice differently.

The literature of pluralism, especially religious pluralism, is growing. My favorite books on pluralism in America include *What It Means to Be an American* by Michael Walzer and *The One and the Many* by Martin Marty. Other important writers in this area include Anthony

Appiah, Will Kymlicka, John Berry, Amy Gutmann, and Charles Taylor. In the specific area of religious pluralism, I find myself constantly referring to Diana Eck's two excellent books on the topic, *Encountering God* and *A New Religious America*. More and more books on the history of religious cooperation are being written. I particularly like Maria Rosa Menocal's *The Ornament of the World*, a set of lyrical vignettes about medieval Andalusia, where Muslims, Christians, and Jews lived together in a spirit of mutual enrichment. There is also a growing literature on the interfaith movement. An excellent history of the movement can be found in Marcus Braybrooke's *Pilgrimage of Hope*. I coedited a volume with Patrice Brodeur, who has played a key role in many interfaith endeavors, called *Building the Interfaith Youth Movement*. The journal *CrossCurrents* has focused on interfaith cooperation for many years, and the journal *Interreligious Insight* also is good.

The social entrepreneurship movement is one of the most exciting new forces of our time. I am honored that the Interfaith Youth Core is considered part of it. David Bornstein's *How to Change the World* is an excellent history of social entrepreneurship and does a particularly good job of articulating its distinctiveness and profiling its founder, Bill Drayton of the organization Ashoka. There are several excellent memoirs by social entrepreneurs on how they started their organizations. Two good recent ones are Wendy Kopp's *One Day, All Children . . .* , on the beginnings of Teach for America, and the Nobel laureate Muhammad Yunus's *Banker to the Poor*, on the founding of the Grameen Bank and the field of microfinance. For examples of older social entrepreneurs, see Saul Alinsky's *Rules for Radicals*, on community organizing, and Jane Addams's *Twenty Years at Hull House*, on the beginnings of the settlement house movement. There is an excellent biography of Alinsky called *Let Them Call Me Rebel* and several good ones of Jane Addams, including one by the theologian Jean Bethke Elshtain.

My greatest inspiration for this book came from the faith heroes who emerged as leaders in their teens and twenties and built movements with profound interfaith character. Chief among these are Nelson Mandela, Dorothy Day, Martin Luther King Jr., and Mahatma Gandhi. Each of them has written a revealing and highly recommended autobiography. In addition, I love Taylor Branch's three-volume set on the civil rights movement, *America in the King Years*, as well as King's collected writings and speeches, *A Testament of Hope*, edited by James Washington. I remember staying up all night in India, aided in my insomnia by a colony of ravenous bedbugs, to finish Louis Fisher's excellent biography of Gandhi. The best-known biography of Mandela is by Anthony Sampson. I also suggest biographies on Abdul Ghaffar Khan (also known as Badshah Khan), a Pashtun Muslim who worked closely with Gandhi to liberate India.

If there is one guiding intellectual behind this book, in both style and vision, it is James Baldwin. The Library of America has compiled a comprehensive collection of his nonfiction into a beautiful volume edited by Toni Morrison. It includes his three most important books —*The Fire Next Time*, *Notes of a Native Son*, and *Nobody Knows My Name*—as well as a number of essays and talks. If I was banished to a desert island and allowed one book in addition to my English translation of the Qur'an, it would be Baldwin's collected nonfiction.